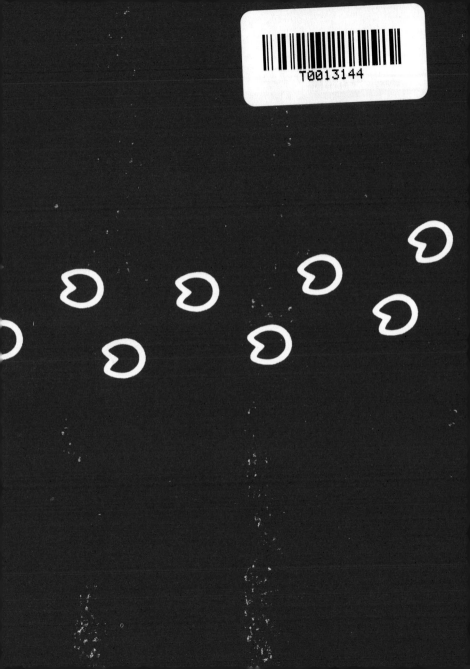

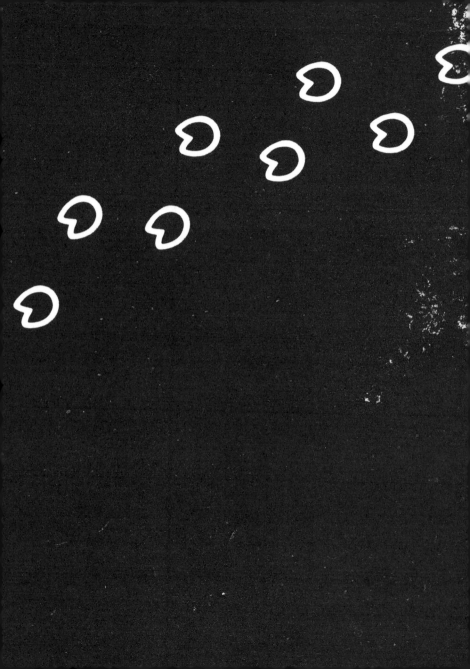

If anyone has exemplified the impactful principles described in this book, it's my friend Rachel Ridge. For two decades, I've had a front-row seat to her life. Each season has been a beautiful illustration of what happens when someone consistently leans in to their personal authenticity, creative capacity, and unique purpose. My own life has been greatly impacted by Rachel. And Flash. And Henry. Through the years, they've each dropped hints about living intentionally, humbly, and deeply. Who knew that a pair of donkeys could do that! This book is fantastic. Every page drew me in—making me smile, reflect, and consider the future. Each chapter is brimming with Rachel's heartfelt personal experience and practical principles that will compel you to ask hard but necessary questions. Then it will catalyze you upward to a higher level—in business, personal relationships, and almost any other aspect of life. So read *The Donkey Principle* with a pen in hand. And then wait a while and read it all over again.

PRISCILLA SHIRER, bestselling author and Bible teacher

I love this book, and you will too. Rachel is us. The lessons she has learned with her two precious donkeys are practical, doable, and hope-filled for the long haul.

SHEILA WALSH, bestselling author

A must-read for everyone who has ever felt like a fuzzy donkey in a field full of shiny thoroughbreds. *The Donkey Principle* offers your soul the permission and encouragement it has been craving. Writing with relatable authenticity and practical applications, Rachel Ridge invites readers to linger in the pasture with her donkeys, Flash and Henry, and imagine a different way of life. A life free from the trap of comparison. A life full of meaning and purpose. And a life that honors and embraces the inner donkey inside all of us.

JENNIFER MARSHALL BLEAKLEY, author of *Joey*, *Project Solomon*, and the Pawverbs devotional series

Fabulous! I will never look at a donkey the same way again. These charming creatures have so much to teach us about how to live, find purpose, and walk with God. And there couldn't be a better guide for your journey than Rachel Anne Ridge.

LISA WHELCHEL, actress and author

As Rachel Anne Ridge says in this extraordinary book, "Precious gold is available to those who are in it for the long haul—who are willing to go deep, time after time, to bring that mother lode from within into the light of day." I may not have made it as a doctor or a lawyer, but for fifty years I've been following the track she describes in this book. My donkey, Little Jack Horner, and I have found that "precious gold" and more joy than I could ever have imagined! Rachel has charted a map to a truly successful and fulfilling life that is so simple, but so rewarding! "Joy happens when we stop pretending to be something we are not, and instead, become the truest version of who we *are*."

MEREDITH HODGES, founder, Lucky Three Ranch

If you've struggled with confidence and comparison, you'll find this book is a breath of fresh air. It gives you permission to embrace the uniqueness of your journey and the strength to forge a path leading to *your* version of success. Approach life with a donkey's keen sense of curiosity and watch the magic happen!

ALISON LUMBATIS, entrepreneur, author, and speaker

The beautiful union between this amazing author and storyteller and her beloved Flash brings a book of life principles that has something for everyone. All of this is inspired by a donkey that teaches us to never underestimate the enlightenment and wisdom we gain when we are open to receiving it in the simplest of forms—like a furry friend!

CINDY OWEN, Given Entertainment

TYNDALE
MOMENTUM®

A Tyndale nonfiction imprint

THE DONKEY PRINCIPLE

THE SECRET TO LONG-HAUL LIVING IN A RACEHORSE WORLD

RACHEL ANNE RIDGE

Visit Tyndale online at tyndale.com.

Visit Tyndale Momentum online at tyndalemomentum.com.

Visit the author online at rachelanneridge.com.

Tyndale, Tyndale's quill logo, *Tyndale Momentum*, and the Tyndale Momentum logo are registered trademarks of Tyndale House Ministries. Tyndale Momentum is a nonfiction imprint of Tyndale House Publishers, Carol Stream, Illinois.

The Donkey Principle: The Secret to Long-Haul Living in a Racehorse World

Designed by Libby Dykstra

Edited by Bonne Steffen

For information about special discounts for bulk purchases, please contact Tyndale House Publishers at csresponse@tyndale.com, or call 1-855-277-9400.

Library of Congress Cataloging-in-Publication Data

A catalog record for this book is available from the Library of Congress.

ISBN 978-1-4964-6037-0

Printed in China

29	28	27	26	25	24	23
7	6	5	4	3	2	1

For Ivy, Heidi, Hazel, August, and Caroline

May you always live your truest,
bravest, and goodest lives.

CONTENTS

FOREWORD

Not too long ago I bought a fifty-year-old youth camp. It smelled like hundreds of junior high school boys had lived there without taking showers. We stripped the walls down to the studs, gave away the bunk beds, cleaned up all of the Skittles we found hidden in small openings in the rooms, and repurposed the buildings to include suites where adults would be comfortable. The last thing we did was acquire an adjacent property and turn it into a farm. I didn't know a thing about farming but right away started collecting animals. We got a couple of everything—chickens, sheep, cattle, pigs, and horses. It felt like we had recreated Noah's wooden ark two by two. I wondered how Noah felt when he let two termites on board his wooden boat before setting sail? Obedience always has a cost.

Most of the people who come to our camp have as little experience around farm animals as I once did. The ones who did know their way around the barn all asked the same question.

"Why don't you have a couple of donkeys?" At first, I thought they were kidding, but I soon learned that a farm without a donkey or two is missing something important. Here's why. Donkeys are sweet and gentle and fiercely loyal to those they trust. They are protective of the other animals and bond deeply with those who surround them. In a word, they exhibit the best characteristics we could hope to see developed in our own lives.

God often drops the most unlikely teachers in our paths. The gift each of us is given in equal shares is the opportunity to listen to them. In this book, you are going to learn a lot more about donkeys than you probably have heard before. When you turn the last page, Rachel isn't hoping you will want to make a hobby farm out of your beautiful life; she hopes you will make it a working ranch. This is not merely the story about a particular donkey; it is a story about you and me—how we can grow and what we might learn about our lives if we're willing.

Welcome to Rachel's ranch.

BOB GOFF

Husband, father, donkey lover,
and author of four New York Times *bestselling books*

Your life
is a gold mine
that's filled
with treasures
just waiting
to be unearthed.

INTRODUCTION

The Boys were waiting for me at the gate. Flash and Henry, my two rescue donkeys, know the drill: If they want to be let into the yard where the "good grass" is (their term, not mine), they have to stand quietly and let me clean their hooves first. In my pocket I had a stash of graham crackers, which I would dole out in bite-sized pieces after each cooperative hoof-lift, but they were already nosing around in hopes of nabbing a pre-snack of their favorite treat.

"You know the rules," I scolded them with a laugh. Henry lined up to be first, his chubby body placed squarely in front of Flash. He was already shifting his weight off his right front leg so I could lift his foot and begin picking the mud out from his hoof with a small metal tool.

"Nice job, pal," I told him as I worked my way around his four hooves. His soft lips tickled my palm as he deftly grasped and crunched the cracker with delight. Henry believed he had done *such* a nice job that he should receive a bonus reward. "You're right, Henry," I said as I broke off another piece. Flash impatiently waited his turn, ears back and lips tightened to show his annoyance at being second in line and the last to receive treats.

"Okay, Flash. Let's have a look at you." I had to catch a plane that morning, but I didn't rush. I ruffled Flash's multi-colored mane and rubbed his shoulders along the distinctive cross-shaped markings. As I cleaned his hooves, I admired how hardy they were, perfectly suited for rocky wilderness treks. I ran my hands down Flash's strong legs and ended the session with the well-earned treat and a final scratch on his rump.

I'd been invited to be a panelist for an event that celebrates women's achievements. Each of us had been asked to present our perspectives on success and share the lessons we'd learned along the way. As strange as it sounds, I owed much of my *own* success to these two donkeys, who were now arguing over the last of the grahams with dramatic ear-shakes and grunts. Their stories and lessons made their way into my books and helped change the trajectory of my career. I'm pretty sure my journey was different from the other panelists', but I also knew that there were many aspects of my unique story that the audience would relate to.

You see, I didn't start my career in art until I was thirty-five, when I picked up a paintbrush for the very first time. It had taken decades for me to work up the courage to try anything creative after my ninth-grade art teacher told me I should drop his class because I had no talent. His crushing remark convinced me that I was no good at the one thing I really wanted to do, which was make art.

Finally, in desperation, I signed up for a craft-painting lesson at my local hobby store. I fell in love with painting and began decorating anything in my house that didn't move—furniture, cabinets, walls, ceilings. Before I knew, it my hobby grew into a twenty-year career as a muralist, surface designer, and creator of original art pieces for residential and corporate clients.

But forging my own creative path was not easy—in fact, it was a hardscrabble fight to survive at times.

I had no art degree or credentials.

No legacy wealth to support my dream.

No business background suitable for this kind of endeavor.

The journey required resilience and resourcefulness, nimble responses to changing needs and economic challenges, humility for learning on the job, and a stubborn streak to stick with it when things got hard.

Flash, my first rescue donkey, had arrived on my driveway (literally) at one of the lowest points in that career. He seemed like an interruption in an already stressful life, but my family and I took him in. I learned that donkeys are the very image of resilience, hard work, service, charm, and loyalty. And over time, I began to view Flash as my own personal model of grit and determination. By embracing my own "inner donkey," I found my way on the rocky trails of this entrepreneurial life and discovered the character and resolve I needed to do meaningful work in the world.

The result? I wrote my first book at age fifty! *Flash: The Homeless Donkey Who Taught Me about Life, Faith, and Second Chances* was surprisingly successful and has even been optioned as a movie. Several books and illustration projects later, my creative path took yet another turn as I began speaking to audiences around the country and life-coaching individuals and groups. It was this unlikely road to living my dream and doing this work that had earned me a spot on the upcoming panel.

A short flight and hotel stay later, I was dressed in the new outfit I had purchased just for this event. As I took my seat on the panel, my excitement grew. The audience in the auditorium quieted and the stage lights came on. As luck would have it, I was the last panelist to be introduced, and that's when my confidence took a hit. My mouth went dry. As each of the other panelists' impressive bios were read, my stomach began to churn and my face flushed. I listened to their impressive lists of educational backgrounds, corporate positions, awards, brokered deals, and prestigious board memberships as I waited for my horribly lackluster bio to be read. WHY had I believed it was beefy enough for this event? In a matter of minutes, my excitement became sheer embarrassment.

I don't belong here.

I feel so dumb.

Dumb, dumb, dumb.

How can I possibly think I fit into this corporate event?

At that moment I wanted nothing more than to sink into a hole on the stage and disappear. With no trapdoor in sight, I tried to think of my options. I could pull the phone from my pocket, raise a finger to indicate an emergency, and run out! *That's it! I'll do that.* My fingers were beginning to curl around the phone when I heard my name and career history being read.

It was too late.

I felt like a shabby donkey among the shiny thoroughbreds on this panel.

Shabby. Slow. Laughable. Unworthy.

Next to the shiny racehorses of the world, my career highlights seemed completely unremarkable, even silly.

I took a deep, shaky breath, and that was when I remembered: *Embrace your inner donkey. Honor the story that brought you here.* I thought about all the people in the audience who had also heard the gold-star biographies and now were comparing them with their own shaggy stories. Perhaps they, too, felt like they didn't measure up. *The haves and the have-nots. The shinies and the shabbies.*

You are my people. We are all doing our best to hide the struggles we've been through, the hard knocks, the hurts and disappointments, and the rock-strewn paths we've had to traverse in order to get here. We all try to position our stories in the best possible light and hope no one asks too many questions or pokes any holes in the accounts. We are tempted to embellish our bios. Somewhere along the way we've bought into the narrative that everyone else has had a smooth ride to get to where they are, while *ours alone* was a meandering shabby donkey of a ride, limping along and barely making it to the finish line. We forget to see the amazing fortitude and grit that it took to navigate the rocky terrain and unmarked path to bring us to our purpose in life.

I looked at the faces of the people in front of me, and I realized that most of us feel like misfits in limbo, waiting for opportunities to live creative, meaningful, and abundant lives. We struggle to imagine what it's like to run free, live joyously, have dreams, and feel the strength of our own power carrying us forward. We want to be better leaders, have deeper relationships, and have a clear sense of purpose, but it seems like those things are for the "haves" and the "shinies." Our social media accounts leave us feeling all too ordinary, completely un-pictureworthy, and entirely drab in comparison to the beautiful influencers in our feeds.

At times, if we're honest, all of us feel like donkeys in a world that celebrates racehorses.

When my turn to speak finally came, I had regained my sense of confidence. Turns out, the truest me didn't need an Ivy League résumé to impact the world. My story brought me full circle back to those donkeys and the power of a simple metaphor to spark imagination. I realized that Flash and Henry were indeed the perfect emblem for creating a more fulfilling life, a better mindset, and success that lasts. Humble, hardworking, resilient, built for difficult paths, and made for drought, donkeys embody the ethic of serving and thriving in tough times. By harnessing the power of my own inner donkey, I had found the strength, determination, excitement, and yes, a bit of stubbornness to achieve the kind of life I'd always wanted . . . and I knew that others could do it too. As I shared my definition of success, I could feel the audience connecting on a near-tangible level.

After the event, people lined up to tell me their own donkey-in-a-racehorse-world stories. Many had tears in their eyes as they shared how much they needed to hear this hope-filled story.

The truth is this: Life isn't a racetrack that's built only for the fastest, shiniest thoroughbreds competing for some elusive prize. Not at all! Instead, life—*your* life—is a gold mine that's filled with treasures just waiting to be unearthed. Precious gold is available to those who are in it for the long haul—who are willing to go deep, time after time, to bring that mother lode from within into the light of day.

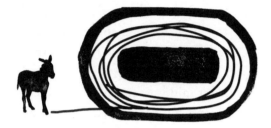

As silly as the idea of a donkey on a racetrack might be, it would be just as ludicrous to put a racehorse to work in a gold mine. As donkeys, we can get off that endless loop of competition to find the kinds of paths and work that suit us best, where we can truly bless the world with our authentic gifts. It's *that* kind of gold that creates wealth in the best sense of the word.

I call this idea "the Donkey Principle," which is this:

WHEN YOU EMBRACE YOUR INNER DONKEY, YOU WILL FIND AND FLOURISH IN THE MEANINGFUL WORK YOU WERE CREATED TO DO.

In other words, quit competing and start digging.

This principle is inspired by the two charming characters in my pasture and their whole equine species, and its framework follows the acronym **GOLD**: **G**ive Yourself Permission, **O**wn Your Story, **L**ean In to Your Unique Strengths, and **D**eliver Your Work. In the pages of this book, you'll read stories of donkeys from history, literature, and modern-day events that I hope will surprise and delight you, and help you remember the concepts they illustrate. For further reflection, I've added "Dig Deeper" questions at the end of each section and lines to jot down "nuggets" you find along the way. These ideas, wrapped up in all my love, are written to remind you of what's truly important. They will help you discover your own stubborn strength, and they'll provide unforgettable inspiration for moving forward with *your* personal definition of success.

The Donkey Principle is the key to living well for the long haul.

GIVE YOURSELF PERMISSION

CHAPTER 1

ASK

The phone on my nightstand wakes me early on a Saturday morning with its insistent buzz. My neighbor's voice sounds apologetic yet strangely amused, but I'm too groggy to tell which.

"Sorry to wake you, Rachel," Priscilla says. "But I'm on my way to work out at the gym and there are a couple of donkeys running loose down the road, and well . . . they look an awful lot like Flash and Henry."

Oh, dear Lord. What on earth?

I rouse my husband, Tom, and within minutes we are dressed and outside, pausing to inspect the pasture as we gather halters and a bucket of sweet feed.

Someone has left the back gate open.

And by "someone" I mean me. It was me. *Me* forgot to close it the night before.

Flash, my rescue donkey, and Henry, the miniature donkey I adopted to keep Flash company, probably didn't notice the mistake until the light of day. But when they did?

No one had to ask them twice.

I imagine Flash, a standard-sized, brownish-gray donkey, glancing over his shoulder at Henry, a chubby, chocolate-colored miniature donkey with a scruffy mane and somewhat silly tail, and then motioning toward the gate with his head.

"Why not?" Henry agrees.

Ears pricked and nostrils flared, they're overcome by curiosity for what lies beyond the gate.

Flash is already out the gate and down the gravel driveway.

"What would it feel like to run free?" he tosses back at the smaller donkey who is hoofing it to keep up.

"Probably a lot like this!" Henry's stubby little legs charge forward, his back end bucking with excitement as if it has a mind of its own.

Through the tunnel of trees and past the pond, the two donkeys on the lam slow to a brisk trot as they approach the blacktop road at the end of the drive.

"What would you like to do?" Henry looks to Flash, as he always does, for leadership.

"We don't have a lot of time," Flash responds with a deep

breath through rubbery lips. It makes a "pphhhht" sound in the still morning air. "We've got to make the most of it!"

Two sets of hooves reach the pavement and turn west as if synchronized. There is a wide, unfenced field a half-mile away from our house, and it beckons them with visions of tall grasses, wildflowers, and maybe even a patch of dirt to roll in. They break into a gallop, ears flapping, tails waving, and flatulence flying—all punctuating their powerful strides with abandon.

I didn't actually see it all happen, but I *know* just how it went down with those jokers. By the time Tom and I reach The Boys, they are wet with perspiration, belly deep in spring foliage, and entirely uninterested in ending their escapade in the wilds of our Texas ranchette neighborhood.

"Live as if someone left the gate open."

The image of the two donkeys making an early dawn break for it—taking a chance on adventure—makes me laugh every time.

Eager.

Reckless.

Driven by curiosity—endless inquisitiveness about absolutely everything.

Living curious—including but not limited to a nose for meddling, a keen interest in all activity in the vicinity, and a penchant for quizzical expressions—is the foundation of the Donkey Principle. Curiosity looks beyond the fences we've placed around our thinking and dares to seek out new information, novel experiences, and outside-the-box solutions. It opens the gate to imagination and long-term excitement for discovery and awe.

Albert Einstein, the physicist who developed the theory of relativity, once said, "The important thing is not to stop questioning. Curiosity has its own reason for existing. One cannot help but be in awe when he contemplates the mysteries of eternity, of life, of the marvelous structure of reality. It is enough if one tries merely to comprehend a little of this mystery every day."

Most of us are not on a quest to discover the laws governing the universe like Einstein was. Perhaps our questions are more along the lines of "What brewing process makes the best cup of coffee?" or "What's for lunch?" Maybe some of us have stopped asking deeper questions of our lives altogether. We keep the curiosity gate closed in order to stay in the comfort zone of our own pastures.

Give yourself permission to be curious. Allow yourself to chase ideas that may challenge you, excite you, and even upend your predictable existence. Asking questions—and then staying with them until the answers arrive—makes all the difference in how your life, your career, and your relationships work.

At its center, top-shelf donkey curiosity involves three simple questions that have the power to discover the gold within you:

Why not?
What would?
And
When will?

WHY NOT?

I looked at the donkey in question. He had appeared out of nowhere, that night on the driveway, and now we had the local sheriff involved. It had been a rescue mission for the history books, with Tom and me pushing, pulling, chasing, and bribing this ornery animal into our pasture.

By the light of day, he seemed like every run-of-the-mill gray donkey I'd ever imagined. Nothing special, nothing noteworthy, except for the deep gashes from a run-in with a barbed wire fence. Long ears, distinctive markings, white muzzle, sad-looking demeanor, much like Eeyore in the Winnie-the-Pooh stories. I could send him packing and be done with it right this moment. I could have moved on from that interruption in my life.

But something about this very ordinary donkey has stolen my heart. Maybe the prospect catches me just at the right moment of indecision, or maybe I notice a tiny flicker of hope in those soft eyes.

"Well, what do you think? You wanna keep him for now?" The sheriff is looking at me, his brushy moustache twitching.

"Oh, why not?" I say. "We'll hang on to him for a while longer, in case his owner shows up to get him."

Why not?

Well, I can think of ten reasons why it isn't a good idea.

We don't have time to care for a beast of burden.

We don't know anything about donkey care.

We probably can't afford it.

Somebody might get hurt by this animal.

I'm not really a "donkey person."

This list is long, but in the end . . . my heart says, *Why not?*

What *do* we have to lose, anyway?

I've found myself facing decisions—both big and small—with the words "no, I can't" on my lips, ready with all the perfectly logical reasons to resist moving forward.

It's not good timing right now.

It will cost too much.

I'm too old to start something new.

I'm not qualified for this new venture.

It's too complicated.

I can't add one more responsibility to my life.

But sometimes, the best answer isn't an answer at all: It's a question.

Why not?

Giving yourself permission to ask *Why not?* frees you to understand that, while the reasons may be logical, they aren't all true. *Why not?* reveals what your intuition is trying to tell you, by poking holes in what appears to be reasonable, realistic, and sensible. It opens you up to possibilities.

And possibilities? Well, those lead to opportunities.

One of the first women to ever receive a patent for an invention was Margaret Knight in 1871. She held a number of factory jobs that suited her technical mind, but she was always thinking of ways to improve the processes. Tasked with the time-consuming and intricate job of folding and gluing paper into bags at a bag company, she wondered, *Why not make a machine that can easily cut and fold bags with square bottoms?* She drew the plans and applied for a patent. Not surprisingly, a man copied her machine and said it was his original idea, but Margaret won the legal battle that followed. Her bag-making machine revolutionized the modern world by mass-producing the simple paper container we still use today. Amazing.

But in 1871? That a woman would have an idea for an invention was nearly unthinkable!

Only it wasn't.

Margaret Knight dared to ask, "Why not?"

The question is not limited to the world of science and industry; it is relevant in every part of life, including music, art, technology, agriculture, parenting, cooking, and personal goal-setting. *Why not* add cardamom to a pot roast? *Why not* imagine a new way to farm? *Why not* let kids sleep in their clothes? *Why not* pursue a degree after you've retired? *Why not* write that book?

You see, *Why not?* finds spaces where others only see obstacles.

Why not? sees windows where others see solid walls.

Why not? sees a donkey who might just be a miracle in disguise.

Why not? finds a gate left open and sees a chance to explore new territory.

Dig Deeper

★ What have you said no to—without first asking yourself, "Why in the world *not*?"

_____

_____

_____

_____

_____

_____

_____

★ What "logical but not true" reasons are holding you back from imagining a new future?

_____

_____

_____

_____

_____

_____

★ When you imagine an abundant future, have you ever asked, "Why not *me*?" *Why not?* often reveals your intuition, your gut feeling, your true intent.

_____

_____

_____

_____

_____

_____

WHAT WOULD?

There is a game called Worst Case Scenario, which, honestly, I could have written the game cards for. Except every solution I'd come up with would have been a form of "PANIC! RUN FOR YOUR LIFE!"

I don't like to think of scenarios of failure or disaster, but that's the way my mind naturally works. At least it did until a friend asked me a powerful question.

We were talking about my creative dreams. I was almost embarrassed to even tell her about them because they sounded so ridiculous. I couched my answer in disclaimers such as "Now this might sound silly" and "I mean, this is just a pipe dream."

My friend listened quietly, then looked me in the eye and said, "Imagine for a moment that you do jump in, and your efforts pay off. What if you get to do all the things you're telling me you want to do? What if you create that course? What if you make that art? What if your creative business grows?"

That's when she dropped the loaded question: "What would that look like for you?"

I was taken aback. Honestly, I'd failed at so many things that it was nearly impossible to picture in my mind what she was suggesting. I blanked out and could not even entertain this fantastical vision of the future. I had to go home and let her words sink in for a while before I could conjure up the image of what success could look like.

Years later, I found myself telling an audience the story of one fateful, dismal night when a stray donkey appeared on my driveway. And I heard myself say these words: "How I wish I could have had a magic button to *flash-forward me into the future* so I could have seen what would happen—right then and there! I would have known just how significant this interruption would be!"

You see, in movies and literature a "flash-forward" is the opposite of a flashback. It's a device in the narrative that inserts a future event or scene into the chronological structure of the work. It can be real, imagined, projected, or expected. This is also known as a *prolepsis*, which comes from a Greek word meaning "anticipation." It is used to give context, meaning, and direction to what is happening in the present.

There on the stage, I experienced a moment of personal insight. My mouth was moving, but my mind was racing back to that conversation with my friend. "What would?" She had asked me to picture a positive future and allow it to shape my present. That night, she had given me a button to flash forward into the future . . . except I hadn't known what to do with it.

I could have saved myself some heartache and trouble if I'd begun to take her suggestion seriously right then and there. I might have hired a personal life coach sooner. I might have let go of projects that didn't propel me toward that dream. I might have even recognized a miracle disguised as a donkey. I could have looked at that unexpected interruption and asked, "What would?" *What would it take for this to be my answer?*

What if you were able to flash forward and see how the things that fill your life right now turn out to be vitally important to your future?

What would you do if you knew your efforts today would be successful someday?

What would your lifestyle be like if your investment pays off?

What would it feel like to be free of the fear of failure?

What would your family be like if you adopted a child?

What would it be like to learn a new language?

What would it be like to know you've made a difference?

What would you do if you could live your ideal life?

What would that look like?

Can you imagine a future for yourself in which you have healthy relationships, abundant resources, personal satisfaction, generous giving, and a rich spiritual life? What would that look like for you?

Right now, I invite you to give yourself permission to be curious about your own future. Look at the activity going on in your life's vicinity and ask yourself, "What would?"

Dig Deeper

★ Write down the following scenario: What would it look like if the dreams you have for your life came true?

WHEN WILL?

Henry paces back and forth along the fence that faces the house. With his ears forward and his mane standing at attention along his neck, he is ready to take on the day. From his vantage point he can see through the glass doors into my kitchen, where the morning's activity is taking place. I shuffle to the coffeepot to pour the magic liquid into my mug and sit down at the table for a few moments of meditation and/or staring off into space (I won't say which). A bray—the squeakiest kind imaginable—pierces the air. Henry has checked with the time clock in his stomach to verify the hour: Breakfast is past due.

Though he can't tell the big hand from the little hand on a clock, Henry has no problem telling time. The pot-bellied, vertically challenged fellow maintains a rigorous schedule:

  8:00 Morning roughhouse with Flash
  9:00 Breakfast of Champions . . . hay, of course
10:00 Nap
11:00 Resume pacing at the fence like a sentinel
12:00 Graze in front pasture
  1:30 Nap

3:00 Free time: browse, snack, nip at Flash for fun
4:00 Nap
5:00 Back to paddock
6:00 Dinner of Champions . . . hay, of course, with
a serving of sweet feed for dessert

Henry gets a little nervous when a wrench gets thrown into the works. Perhaps I have to be gone for the day and there is no outing to the front pasture, or perhaps seasonal grass is so plentiful there is no need for the extra hay. The pacing picks up, and there is the possibility of a gastrointestinal event of the explosive kind. (Henry has issues.)

Thankfully, there is even-keeled Flash, who takes anomalies in the schedule in stride. His unflappable demeanor has a calming effect on Henry, who belatedly realizes that the world won't stop turning if things are off by an hour, or an afternoon. Still, Flash does thrive when there is a predictable pattern in motion, and Henry is the one who helps set that agenda.

"When will?" is the question Henry lives by. Having a schedule helps him stay on top of his responsibilities as tiny Lord of the Paddock and gives him clear direction when life feels out of control. I do *so* admire that.

As a creative artist and writer, I buck against having a schedule or setting a deadline. After all, I might not know when my artistic juices will be flowing or for how long. It might be better to go with the flow, to be open to the winds of inspiration . . . I mean for maximum productivity, right?

Except that "the flow" tends to get bumped by doctor's appointments, needy children, someone else's projects that only I can help with, an extra episode of that series I'm into on Netflix, a last-minute trip to the grocery store, and the flower bed that suddenly needs weeding. Not to mention the silverware drawer is frightfully disorganized. *Who runs this place, anyway?* All of it clamors for attention at precisely the time I had vaguely thought I might sit down to work on my project.

When will?

The answer, of course, is to get specific.

When will I finish? Set a date.

When will lunch be? Set a time.

When will this manuscript be due? Sooner than I think.

When will I put my dreams on a calendar? Today. Today o'clock I will do that.

Scheduling dreams is the stuff of superheroes, titans, and donkeys like Henry. Routines keep us sane in the face of enormous challenges and personal stress. They are the difference between success and failure, achievement and disappointment. (Okay, it helps to have unflappable friends like Flash to encourage you when things go off the rails, but that's not my point here.)

My point is that nailing down the "When will?" is the very thing that turns the opportunity you found when you asked,

"Why not?" and the vision you had when you asked, "What would?" into a beautiful reality.

Benjamin Franklin famously knew the power of a daily schedule. His day included time for self-improvement, work, rest, and the enjoyment of friendships. The inventor, thinker, and philosopher saw that his ideas needed the structure that a calendar provided in order to leave the drawing board and become realities.

Asking (and then answering) "When will?" is *donkey-bold*. It means you're finally taking your dream seriously enough to give it proper real estate on your calendar.

Dig Deeper

★ Take out your planner, or open up your calendar app, and answer the question "When will?"

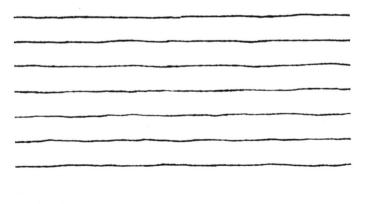

★ Choose a date for finishing that project you're dreaming about.

★ I will finish _____ on this date:
_____.

★ My Lord of the Paddock daily routine is:

_____

_____

_____

_____

_____

_____

_____

_____

_____

_____

_____

_____

_____

"Live as if someone
left the gate open."

—FLASH AND HENRY

CHAPTER 2

ASPIRE

The gilded doors to the Gasparini Room in the royal palace of Spain's King Charles III part in unison, opened by the two uniformed pages stationed on either side. It is 1784, just a few short years after the American Revolution.

"The Count of Floridablanca," intones the king's secretary as the Spanish Minister of State steps into the room. His heels echo on the floral-patterned mosaic floor, making the ornate chamber feel even grander, if it were possible. He pauses below the enormous chandelier which hangs from the center of the painted ceiling, bows, and waits for King Charles III to motion him forward.

When he glances at his appointment book, the king sees the Minister of State's name there: "Requesting a personal favor for

General George Washington." The king nods knowingly. He is accustomed to personal requests by world leaders. The savvy ruler of Spain has consolidated power and deftly dealt with international negotiations, and is curious why his Minister of State is approaching him on Washington's behalf. The king's mind quickly runs through the possible favors: a countryside villa, perhaps? Spanish marble for Washington's personal residence? A secret military alliance of some kind? A sizable loan? Intrigued, he sits back in his velvet chair and waits.

After exchanging formal pleasantries for several moments, the Minister of State gets to the point.

"Your Majesty, according to our law, many items exclusive to Spain are prohibited from being exported. The chargé d'affaires from the United States has brought to my attention that General Washington has, for the past four years, sought to import one of those items to America . . . but thus far has been unsuccessful."

King Charles III leans forward. "What does he want?"

The Minister of State clears his throat.

"Donkeys, sir. The General would like a pair of donkeys."

"Ahh," the king rubs his chin, beginning to smile. "The donkeys, of course." Spain's Cordovan donkeys are so renowned for their size, strength, and beauty that he has insisted on keeping them as an asset contained within his own country's borders. Obtaining one for export requires a royal exemption which he alone can give. He lets the request hang in the air for dramatic effect, then waves his right hand.

"Tell the chargé d'affaires I will be happy to oblige General Washington. I will personally select two of our finest donkeys and have them sent with royal handlers to the port of his choice," he said. The General could have asked for just about *anything*, no matter how difficult to obtain or how expensive the price tag, and he would have granted it. And yet, what he wants is donkeys—Spanish donkeys.

George Washington promptly sets about making meticulous arrangements for the receipt of the two exquisite animals he has long sought. Much to his disappointment, only one donkey survives the voyage. Each detail of the monthslong travel by foot (and hoof) from the port of Gloucester, Massachusetts, to Boston to Mount Vernon, Virginia, is overseen by his right-hand man, John Fairfax. Royal Gift, as Washington names the donkey, will be the foundation for a new breed of American animal that he dreams will revolutionize farming and industry, and put the new country on the map as an economic powerhouse.

It seems charming, to our modern sensibilities, that a studly donkey from Spain could be seen as a technological advancement for industry. George Washington had high aspirations for Royal Gift, and through breeding combinations with American draft horses, he helped produce mules and donkeys that could plow up to sixteen acres in a single day—a feat unheard of at the time.

They could haul heavy loads on minimal food and water, with a stamina that made people marvel. His revered donkeys indeed held the promise of "what could be" in the new age of idealism and enlightenment. As they churned up the Western frontier into farmland and built railroads and cities, they came to represent the iconic spirit of integrity, hard work, and optimism—characteristics that will never be outdated or forgotten.

What's my takeaway from this page in history? In order to live fully—to fulfill the promise of "what could be"—we need to give ourselves permission to have those same *wild aspirations*. I call it being our truest, goodest, and bravest selves.

This is the truest thing about you:
You are enough, and you are worthy.

You are worthy of being loved.

You are worthy of having beautiful relationships.

You are worthy of good things coming your way.

You are worthy of being seen and heard.

You are worthy of running with those racehorses.

You are worthy of standing tall in your donkey-self.

Your truest you is the one who sleeps untroubled, who wakes hopeful, who embraces the imperfections of life with grace, and who contains a deep well of wisdom to meet your challenges.

Your truest you is a fully integrated being whose inner self matches the outer self. You are enough.

Your value is intrinsic. Your worth is beyond measure. Your heart beats with the thought *I belong here. This life is mine. I am worthy of living it fully.*

———————

"Nobody wants a donkey like this," the sheriff told me all those years ago when the stray donkey showed up. "If I take him into custody, I probably can't even give him away." He cleared his throat. "Ma'am, I hate to tell you this, but donkeys like this one end up on trucks heading for a black market for their skins— literally making them worth more dead than alive."

But those soft brown eyes told me a different story. Looking into them, I saw something that touched my heart, something warm, something that hinted at a soul that was sad and lost and waiting. He was simply hoping for someone to see his worth and bring him home.

What is true of Flash the donkey is true of you.

You were valuable before anyone ever recognized your worth. Even before you took your first breath, you were created for goodness—not for "achievement," but for *presence* that comes from deep within. A knowing, a sureness, a trueness that you belong in this world, and you are worthy of your place here.

You *can* sleep untroubled. You *can* wake hopeful. You *can* live confidently each day. You can meet your challenges with wisdom and kindheartedness. Why? Because your truest you has everything you need to flourish, to discover the gold deep inside you, and to see your wild aspirations come true.

We all spend an inordinate amount of time vying to compete on the racetrack of career and personal advancement. We pretend to be slick and shiny, built for speed and fame—all the while knowing deep inside that this is not who we really are. Pretending only gives us a false sense of belonging. When we finally embrace our true donkey-selves, we begin to belong on our own terms.

Brené Brown puts it this way: "True belonging is the spiritual practice of believing in and belonging to yourself so deeply that you can share your most authentic self with the world and find sacredness in both being a part of something and standing alone in the wilderness. True belonging doesn't require you to *change* who you are; it requires you to *be* who you are."

The truest thing about you is that you are worthy of all the love, all the dancing, all the belonging, and all the goodness this world has to offer.

You are enough.

Dig Deeper

★ Why not name one thing that is true about you that you keep hidden from others?

_____

_____

_____

_____

_____

★ What would it look like for you to be fully authentic as a person? As a leader? As a friend?

_____

_____

_____

_____

_____

★ When will you embrace your "inner donkey"?
Date: _____

GOODEST

Stop trying to live your best life.

That seems counterintuitive, right? Of course you should try to live your best life!

Or should you?

We are always being urged to "Live Your BEST Life Now." You need to have the best job, drive the best car, have the best things, maintain the best body. Live every moment in the best way possible.

It's fabulous! It's the BEST!

But honestly? It's exhausting.

Listen, being the best is overrated.

So, what if you went for something else entirely?

You see, in your quest to be best, it's easy to forget how to simply be *good*.

Once, as a discouraged mother of teenagers, I sat alone in my bedroom wiping away tears. Conflict over something important I'd forgotten to do made me retreat behind my door as I berated myself for failing yet again. Absentmindedly, I opened a dresser drawer and found an old diary, long abandoned. As I leafed through the pages, I stopped at one entry and tears began to fall once more, but this time for an entirely different reason. A few scrawled lines recounted a moment from years before when I pulled a red wagon with my then two-year-old son to the park. The sun was shining, the birds were singing, and the little blond boy sat in the wagon as we rattled down the sidewalk. Suddenly his tiny voice piped up. "Mommy, you're the goodest mom I ever seen."

His words stopped me in my tracks.

Goodest mom.

Reading those words from so long ago I realized I'd been trying so hard to be the best mom ever, that I'd forgotten the importance of simply being the goodest one. I didn't have to try to control every situation. I didn't have to strive to be perfect. I could let go of all that and lean in to the goodness of my family, in all its flaws and failures. I was free to embrace my mistakes and learn from them, rather than beat myself up over making them in the first place.

I set the old diary down and looked through the window to the pasture beyond. I could see Flash grazing on a patch of clover, content and unhurried. He looked up when his new friend Henry approached and sank his nose into the juicy green treats right next to Flash, and I thought for sure he'd chase the interloper off with a snort or a shove. There wasn't enough for both of them, after all. Flash is the best at finding and maintaining pasture territories . . . and this was *his* spot. Instead, Flash made room with a step to the side, and the donkeys—nose to nose—feasted on the coveted clump.

"Good donkey," I whispered. *He's just the goodest.*

You see, only one person can be the best at something. Their moment of glory is fleeting, and then someone else stands ready to take their place at the top.

But good? Oh, good never goes away. It never goes out of style. No one can ever take away that crown.

This world needs the good you have to offer.

Be a good friend.

Be a good neighbor.

Be a good parent.

Be a good son.

Be a good daughter.

Be a good worker.

Be a good leader.

Being good means that you look out for the needs of others. You find ways to inspire kindness and joy. You bring light and life everywhere you go.

This proved true for a man named Tom Shadyac, who was living "his best life" in Hollywood, successfully directing films such as *Ace Ventura* and *The Nutty Professor*. However, a bicycle accident in 2007 compounded a sense he'd had for some time that life as he lived it was empty. So he decided to trade in his fame and fortune for a mobile home and a bike . . . and a commitment to share what he had with others. He is living his goodest (and happiest) life, enjoying a creative career while helping people along the way. Tom has discovered the secret of leaving space for generosity and kindness.

These days, good is underrated. Good is actually better than best.

Good leaves room for falling down, for the unexpected, for grace. It understands that some of life's most priceless gifts are wrapped in ordinary packages. It gives permission for being kind to yourself and to others.

Don't let your desire to be the best rob you of the goodness that's all around you or take away your ability to do good in the moment.

Stop trying to live your best life.

Live your *goodest* life instead.

Dig Deeper

★ Why not make a list of ways to let go of perfectionism and the need to "be the best," and ask yourself, "Why not try it?"

★ What would a "goodest" life look like for you?

_____

_____

_____

_____

_____

_____

★ When will you do one simple "good thing" for someone?
Write down the first ideas that come to mind.

_____

_____

_____

_____

_____

_____

★ Then set a date here: _____

Your bravest self is willing to try again.

"Come on, buddy. You can do it. You've got this." I call softly to Flash and shake the bucket of oats to encourage him.

Flash stands at the edge of the covered breezeway and looks at me with his deep brown eyes. His gaze falls to the cement floor as he ponders the gravity of his next move. He will have to step up and onto the smooth surface in order to walk across to where I am holding the delicious reward.

I wait while he deliberates. It seems like such a simple thing: walking through the porch area just like his two-legged people do all the time.

But to a donkey? It's not so simple.

Being asked to step onto an unfamiliar surface is unnerving, scary. A change, say from grass to gravel, or from dirt to pavement, is a huge statement of trust in the one who is leading him forward.

A donkey naturally fears losing his footing.

Losing your footing means loss of control.

It means becoming vulnerable to attack, looking weak, feeling uncertain.

Not unlike how *we* approach change.

An unexpected variation in our landscape—being laid off from a job, a new marital status, a move to a different part of the country, or simply being presented with new information that challenges what we believe—makes us want to stop in our tracks out of fear. What lies ahead? What will the future hold? Will the ground hold me or give way beneath me? What is my exit strategy?

Bravery calls us to step forward. It holds forth the reward of personal growth, new mind shifts, and fresh opportunities. Bravery asks us to trust. Often, we find ourselves at the threshold trying to summon the courage for that first step.

Flash takes a tentative step into the breezeway, eyes riveted on the bucket in my hands. Some gravel from the walkway outside sticks to the bottom of his hooves and causes his second step to slip. He tries to catch himself but it is too late, and his legs splay in all directions like a cartoon character before stabilizing. Nostrils flared, he looks at me as if to say, "I knew this was a bad idea!"

Flash clatters backwards, his powerful muscles trembling, his hind legs feeling for the step down as he makes a hasty exit, tail tucked and ears bent low. He is traumatized by this venture, and I know it will take several more tries for him to regain enough confidence to even stand at the step once again. This failure will play mind games now—forever reminding him how dangerous it is to venture into the unknown.

When our own first steps are met with anything less than success, it is tempting to turn tail and hide. It helps to remember that most of the high achievers we revere have experienced failure along the road to their eventual success. Abraham Lincoln, for example, is often cited for overcoming obstacles before he became President. As a child, he spent more time working to help support his family than he did in formal schooling. Later, he knew the sting of business failures and crushing debt, as well as the loss of several bids for congressional office. His path to the White House was not an easy one, yet he persevered to become one of America's most renowned presidents.

Bettye LaVette, considered by the *New York Times* as "one of the best jazz interpreters of her generation," did not see success until later in life. Though she recorded hit songs in the 1960s and 70s, somehow contracts always seemed to fall through or record labels never properly promoted her. Nonetheless, she continued to sing and tour where she could and finally had a breakthrough in the early 2000s. She was "rediscovered" in France when a producer dug through some thought-to-be-long-lost cassette tapes, and a new recording of her song, "Let Me Down Easy" was released. Her perseverance over decades has resulted in a career that now includes two Grammy nominations, television appearances, concerts, and music awards. Now in her seventies, Ms. LaVette's willingness to keep on trying is inspirational to all.

Bravest is choosing to walk across uncertain ground for the reward on the other side. Bravest is summoning the courage to do it scared. Sometimes the reward is a bucket of oats, sometimes it's a new opportunity, sometimes it's the pride of personal accomplishment. But bravest is the thing that says, "I will try again."

Flash eventually learned to cross the breezeway like a pro. It took several attempts for him to work up the courage to trust his own footing, but when he finally did, he walked with head held high and ears waving like banners . . . straight to the oats.

Be your bravest self. You have everything you need to move forward.

Dig Deeper

★ Why not name the fear that's holding you back?

_____

_____

_____

_____

_____

★ What would it look like to live without that fear?

_____

_____

_____

_____

_____

_____

_____

_____

_____

_____

★ When will you take that first step toward trying again?
  Date: _____

OWN
YOUR STORY

CHAPTER 3

ASCRIBE HONOR

"Wake up, Estelle! Today is the day!"

The girl yawns sleepily from under her thick quilts. At fourteen, Estelle is accustomed to waking early to milk the goats and tend the fire, but there is an excitement in her mother's voice that causes her to sit up and remember why this day is special. It is January 14, 1512, and her small French village is already bustling with preparation for the Feast of the Asses, a celebration of the biblical donkeys, especially the donkey ridden by Mary as she fled with Joseph and the baby Jesus to Egypt. Estelle, the prettiest girl in town, has been chosen to play the part of Mary in a reenactment through the town streets that will culminate with a special mass at the church and a bountiful feast.

Dressed in a blue woolen dress with a cream-colored cloak over her shoulders, Estelle perches atop a small gray donkey named Cleo who is festooned with ribbons in his mane and tail. Cleo, a veteran of past festivals, waits patiently for the elaborate procession to begin. A wriggling bundle is placed into Estelle's arms—her baby nephew will play Jesus—and then they are off down the cobblestone street toward the square. Estelle feels nervous at the thought of the cheering crowds lining the way, but as they round the first corner all anxiety melts away. That's when she remembers that *she* is not the center of attention today.

This celebration is all about the donkey.

Cleo's ears swivel around at the sound of Estelle's voice as she pats him gently with one hand while cuddling the babe with the other. The crowd presses in, ringing bells and singing the song sung for centuries:

"From the Eastern Lands came a lordly ass of highest fame, so beautiful, so strong and trim, no burden was too great for him. Hail, Sir Donkey, hail."

Cleo seems bemused by all the attention. Up the steps of the church and into the sanctuary, the burro clops forward until he reaches the altar where a well-rehearsed play unfolds. As if on cue, he shakes his ears and brays, the plaintive sound filling the stone chapel and causing the congregants to erupt in laughter. One by one, characters come forward to pay homage: three wise men present gifts, shepherds bow low, women hang wreaths around the donkey's neck. Cleo stands front and center, ears forward and head cocked sideways, taking it all in.

"Today we ascribe honor to the donkey who brought the Lord Jesus to safety," the priest begins his homily. "We remember his service, and we give thanks for God's humble creature who carried the Divine Story on his back." As a young boy playing the part of a shepherd scratches Cleo's ears, the priest recounts stories of other donkeys in the Bible: Balaam's donkey, the Christmas donkey, and the young foal Jesus rode into Jerusalem on Palm Sunday. All were important players in the grand history of divine love. Finally, he ends the homily, not with his usual "Amen," but with three loud brays of his own: *"Hinham, hinham, hinham!"*

"Hinham, hinham, hinham!" the congregation responds, nearly falling off their pews in raucous delight. At this, the baby begins to wail, and Cleo trots toward the exit, with Estelle hanging on to the baby (and Cleo's mane) for dear life—ribbons and festoons flying behind. He bolts toward the tables in the courtyard, which are piled high with fresh breads and dried fruits for the feast. Skidding to a stop in front of the fountain, the guest of honor nabs a carrot that's rolling off a table and munches away to the cheers of the crowd.

The medieval Feast of the Asses was a celebration that ascribed honor to the humble creatures who brought the Divine Story on their backs. When we ascribe honor as a way of life, it reminds *us* to live humbly, in gratitude for the unsung people and circumstances that have brought us here. Any success we might achieve—and anything of lasting value that we treasure—arrives not because of our own efforts alone. It takes a community of people to build a history of both successes and failures, to bring a dream to fruition. That's why the best leaders, thinkers, and creators are those who live out this kind of humility. They know the power of ascribing honor where it's due.

We do well to honor the "donkeys" who have helped carry our *own* divine stories: our past, our present, and our people.

YOUR PAST

Ascribe honor to the past that brought you here.

Your history, however humble, deserves a place at the altar where it can receive the proper acknowledgment for its role in your current life. It can be difficult to stand quietly by as you recount the stories that played a part in who you have become. Perhaps, like Cleo, you feel uncomfortable in a place of sacred Presence, and you can't help but let out a nervous bray in response. Sometimes we make jokes or try to deflect attention as a defense mechanism against the shame that bubbles up through the gravitas of the moment.

I shouldn't be here, you might be thinking. *I don't belong.* But remember, this is an entire Feast of the Asses, a moment in time to recognize the "absurdity" of donkeys having an impact and making their mark on the world.

Ascribing honor to our past doesn't mean that we celebrate every part of it. Indeed, it may be too painful to relive the details that have caused us mental, physical, emotional, or spiritual anguish. What it *does* mean is that we own our history, both the good and the bad. We give place to the parts of our story that nurtured and helped us grow, while holding space for the dark corners where hurts may haunt us. Ascribing honor doesn't *fix* the past, but it provides a way of viewing it that moves us beyond shame and unresolved pain toward healing and growth.

"Leave the past behind" is a common piece of advice, or as Pumba says in *The Lion King*, "Put your behind in the past." That's easier said than done. Often, we find ourselves stuck in old patterns, memories, and hurts that keep us from moving forward in our lives. Rather than trying to forget your past, honoring it grants you the freedom to visit.

———

My friend Jenny's childhood was marked by instability. Raised by a single parent who struggled with addiction, Jenny took it upon herself to make sure her younger siblings had clean clothes to wear to school and did their homework at night. Jenny was popular at school, but she never invited any friends over because she was too embarrassed. She became so adept at hiding her personal life that when she became an adult, she almost convinced herself of an alternate story about her past—a carefree childhood filled with adventure and fun. But by the time she finished college and landed her first job, an overwhelming sense of sadness sometimes kept her from getting out of bed in the morning. She berated herself for not being able to "get it together" and be confident and carefree like everyone else. The more she tried to fit in with her young professional friends, the more miserable she became.

One day, after watching some children ride their bikes with joyful abandon through a park, her tears began to flow. When she couldn't stop crying, she knew it was time to seek help.

Jenny found a therapist who helped her unpack the story she'd kept locked inside. Even though it was difficult, she opened up about her past and something began to shift inside. By sharing her story she began to own it, and the shame she'd carried for so long slowly started to lift. For the first time, she was able to see her past in a new light and offer kindness to the girl who once held it all together, instead of judging the woman who just couldn't do it any longer.

Shame keeps us from believing that we are worthy of living to our fullest potential and inhibits our ability to imagine the beautiful gold we can bring to the world. Of all the things that can keep us stuck, shame takes top prize for shuttering our minds to hope and to limitless thinking.

Like a donkey in a church, the past is made sacred by telling the stories, honoring what you lived, endured, and survived. The past brought to the altar stands as a testament to resilience; the juxtaposition of pain in a holy place gifts us with the tenderness we need to offer ourselves. It makes space for a joy to break through and echo to the rafters that you are here, you have arrived, and you are alive.

Dig Deeper

★ Why not take a bird's-eye view of your past and explore how your experiences have shaped and prepared you for this present moment? Write down any insights that come to mind.

_____

_____

_____

_____

_____

_____

_____

★ What would it feel like to ascribe honor to the past, even the parts that have kept you from embracing new possibilities? What would your life look like if you were able to honor the resilience and strength your past experiences have given you?

_____

_____

_____

_____

_____

_____

_____

_____

_____

★ When will you acknowledge the gifts the past has provided? Consider creating a private ceremony to honor them.
Date: _____

YOUR PRESENT

You are here.

You are alive.

You have arrived at the altar of celebration for this very moment.

Now. It's good to take a breath and *be present* to your present.

Close your eyes for a minute and imagine your present being festooned with wreaths of flowers and ribbons as a ceremonial thanksgiving for simply being here.

Inhale.

Exhale. *Ahhhh.*

I can almost smell the roses and honeysuckle around my neck. What about you?

Henry David Thoreau wrote, "The meeting of two eternities, the past and future, . . . is precisely the present moment." Perhaps there should be a thunderclap—or an actual Feast of the Asses—at such an intersection. Instead we are loading the dishwasher (hey, it's not going to load itself), or scrolling on social media, or simply passing *through* the present moment preoccupied by the future or distracted by the clamor of our times. We are certainly not accustomed to thinking about two eternities meeting while sorting socks and trying to figure out why that grass stain is still on your child's jersey even though you used bleach. Right now is often so mundane and forgettable.

Ascribing honor to the present is a simple practice of mindfulness. It is an intentional act of creating space for gratitude for each breath, for the ground beneath our feet, and for the opportunities that stand ready for us to embark upon. And that can happen even when we are going about the everyday activities of our lives. It's an acknowledgement of the gift of now. It's what my donkeys Flash and Henry do best: They fully appreciate each moment, every mouthful of fresh grass, and each ray of sunshine as it comes.

I remember an incident when my oldest daughter, Lauren, was a toddler. I had dressed her in her playclothes for the day and then lifted her onto the bathroom counter so I could gather her fine red hair into a tiny ponytail on top of her head, Pebbles Flintstone style. With the ponytail secured, I set the comb and spray bottle down, and we wrapped our arms around each other tightly, swaying back and forth. I looked into her bright blue eyes, and we held each other's gaze for a long, long while. *I want to hold this in my memory forever*, I thought. *This girl, this red hair, this little apartment . . . everything.* I breathed it all in, and I knew that Lauren was sharing this intimate connection with her mommy in a special way too.

Just then, my daughter murmured, "I can see the boogies in your nose."

Yes, it was indeed a moment I will never forget, because she was living her *own* moment of discovery, even as I lived mine.

Ascribing honor to the present is a posture of humility and gratitude that uncovers a treasure trove of rewards: It relieves stress and cultivates peace, creates a more positive mindset for solving problems, lowers blood pressure, gives us a sense of groundedness, and helps us gain much-needed perspective, says Dr. Robert Emmons, one of the world's leading scientific experts on gratitude.

Being mindful of the present doesn't try to create magical moments out of the mundane or attempt to force meaning into every single minute, but it does celebrate the life that *allows* for the mundane to exist by placing a "thinking of you" bouquet upon the day's contents. It creates an atmosphere of abundant living that infuses both sock-sorting and deal-signing with a sense of gratitude instead of entitlement. Ascribing honor to the meeting place of eternity past and eternity future finds a sacred home within a sanctuary filled with a community that's present with you.

Dig Deeper

★ What is keeping you from ascribing honor to a day that is filled with mundane tasks and seemingly unimportant details? Be honest.

_____

_____

_____

_____

★ What would it look like to infuse your present with gratitude? What are you most thankful for?

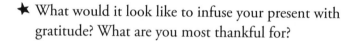

_____

_____

_____

_____

★ When will your present ever be good enough to cause you to celebrate it? Why not celebrate today? Date: _____ I celebrated by

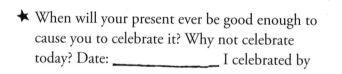

_____.

YOUR PEOPLE

Honor those who have made a way for you.
After all, a celebration isn't complete without a community of individuals who helped make it happen!

From the street sweepers to the flower arrangers, the meal makers to the participants in the play, it took the entire village to pull off the Feast of the Asses. As little Cleo munched on a stolen carrot to the delight of the crowd, each person involved felt the pride of seeing their local donkey being honored in this way. They shared the triumph of the moment as "one of their own" was the star of the day.

I love watching the Academy Awards ceremony each year, as much for the celebrity fashion as for the movies I'm rooting for. The Oscar recipients, often overcome with emotion, try to thank all the people who made their journey to this moment possible before the theme music begins to play and stage attendants usher them offstage. The actors express gratitude for fellow cast members, directors, agents, parents, spouses, and children—all the people that you'd expect—but most poignant of all are the stories that are told . . . of teachers, mentors, parents, and friends who long ago made indelible impacts. Perhaps it was a teacher who encouraged a hidden talent, or a decision maker who said yes early on to an unknown actor, or someone who believed in a story so much that they mortgaged their future on it to make a dream come true.

No one achieves success alone. That's true for an Oscar winner, a Fortune 500 CEO, an artist, a parent, or hey, any and all of us. It always takes a village to create something worthwhile.

Think back through your own journey, and you will recall the names and faces of people who've had a hand in your life. Perhaps you can even remember what you wore on that day or the very words you heard that impacted you greatly. My husband recalls the seasons and the weather conditions wrapped around particular deep-rooted moments in his life, while I tend to remember simply how those influential people made me feel.

An article in the *Harvard Business Review* points out that the most impactful act leaders and managers can do is acknowledge the work of their employees or team members. Recognizing the contributions of others is a powerful force in motivating and creating a positive environment. This kind of humility is the hallmark of great leadership and fosters an atmosphere of mutual respect and cooperation.

Ascribing honor to your people acknowledges those who have added value to your life, or who offer support, encouragement, and belief in the work you are called to do and the person you are becoming. When they look at you, they don't see "just a donkey"; they see someone who has important work to carry out, someone who has the strength and resilience to impact the world, and someone whose calling is worthy of celebration.

Dig Deeper

★ If you are a leader, why not take the time to acknowledge the people who work to make your leadership possible? Begin by noting who they are and how they contribute to your success.

★ What would your life look like if the people who invested their time, interest, support, and encouragement in you hadn't been there for you? How would your current project and work be impacted if you tried to "go it alone"?

★ When will you write thank-you notes to ascribe honor to three people who have helped you succeed? Who are those people and what will you say? Jot down ideas that come to mind here. Then make the notes a priority this week.

CHAPTER 4

ASSUME

I settle cross-legged on the green-and-gold shag carpet as Jiminy Cricket croons, "When You Wish upon a Star."

As a child growing up in the sixties and seventies, I am being raised by parents who worry about the effects of sitting too close to the television on their kids' eyesight (the radiation!), as well as the influence of programs like *Rowan & Martin's Laugh-In* and *The Dick Cavett Show*. We did not have a TV at our house for many years, but on this Sunday night we kids luck out when a church board meeting takes place at our pastor's house, where there is a *color* TV! The meeting goes long into the night—long enough for us to watch the entire film *Pinocchio*, the animated Disney classic from 1940. It tells the legend of a wooden marionette, guided by a cricket as his conscience, who must prove himself worthy to become a real boy.

As the movie begins and a fairy shows up to cast a spell on the little puppet, I just know things will turn out right. But right off the bat, things take a turn for the worse, and the stuff of nightmares begins for generations of unsuspecting children, including me.

Pinocchio's misadventures eventually lure him to Pleasure Island, where boys can be as naughty as they want: smoking cigars, drinking beer, brawling, and destroying property. Shooting billiards? Those boys are really pushing the boundaries toward complete anarchy.

"Give a boy enough rope and he'll soon make a jackass of himself," pronounces the coachman as he drops Pinocchio and his new friend off at the gate. And that's the catch: The magic of doing whatever they want gradually turns them into actual *donkeys*. Dark, apelike creatures appear with the express purpose of throwing the crying donkeys into cages to be sold into slavery in the mines or a life of humiliation in a circus—the only fitting ends for bad donkeys.

Meanwhile, our wooden boy, Pinocchio, begins his life of debauchery but manages to escape the island before his transformation from delinquent to donkey is complete. His long ears and tail are evidence that he has made one bad decision after another, and he remains like this until the final redemptive scene of the movie. Walt Disney is following the storyline of a traditional Italian tale, creating a world of anarchy filled with bad boys who become donkeys. In the Italian culture of the times, the donkey symbolizes ignorance, stupidity, silliness, and labor.

Could there be any more appropriate animal for Pinocchio to become? In this instance, Disney plays upon the assumptions the audience *already has* about donkeys—that they are stupid, obstinate, mean, laughable, selfish, and meant only for slavery or a circus—to make a powerful metaphor about Pinocchio. *Pinocchio is entirely unworthy of becoming a real boy.*

Pinocchio is nothing but a "jackass," just as the conductor prophesied.

While the story ends with Pinocchio becoming a real boy, there is a hidden lesson here: Caricatures like bad-boy donkeys may make for a good laugh in the moment, but they ultimately perpetuate harmful stereotypes. These stereotypes become "facts" in people's minds—or rather, false assumptions. Ask anyone what a donkey is like, and you'll likely hear echoes of Pinocchio in people's responses: stupid, obstinate, mean. They jump to conclusions about a donkey's character based on a hidden bias that they aren't even aware they have.

We all have unconscious biases like this, which are "attitudes or stereotypes that affect our understanding, actions, and decisions in an unconscious way, making them difficult to control."

Our brains seem to be wired to leap to assumptions before our conscious minds can corral our thoughts into a better, more reasoned approach.

It's important to take the time to examine our own assumptions about others and ourselves. If we are to think of our lives as gold mines containing hidden treasure, we must also realize that a lot of rubble must be removed in order to find that gold. Assumptions can be as hard as granite to break apart and sift through, but the reward is worth it.

Assumptions fall into three categories of action: don't assume, never assume, and always assume.

DON'T ASSUME

False assumptions about others build walls of mistrust.

Quickly, fill in the following blanks. Do it as fast as you can without overthinking. Just put down the first thing that comes to mind:

Owls are _____.
Spiders are _____.
Snakes are _____.

Lions are _____.
Donkeys are _____.

Now let's reflect on what you wrote.

Are your snap answers based on personal experience? Have you had more than one interaction with any of the above? What do you know about these creatures from literature? What did your parents say about them? What did you learn about the animals in your culture?

Most of the time, our instant opinions come from somewhere deep in our unconscious mind. We likely never "decided" to think that owls are wise, but if we consider our first encounters with owls, Winnie-the-Pooh's friend Owl might come to mind. A connection was made long before we consciously thought about whether or not an owl has wisdom.

It turns out, much of what we know about individual species comes from folklore, movies, family stories, and what we heard growing up. Chances are, if your father loved snakes, you have an affinity for them too. If your mother screamed when she saw a spider, you may find yourself with the same irrational fear. This "unconscious bias" is something we all have.

But listen up. Unconscious bias toward creatures must stop! Snakes are good! Spiders are beneficial! Owls are . . . okay, okay, this might be a simplistic way to illustrate a point, but it's far more comfortable than talking about how our false assumptions hurt *people*.

Several years ago, my own biases were revealed in a way that shocked me. I was attending a wedding where I didn't know many people other than the bride. I found a table where two ladies were seated and asked if I could join them. One of the women was elderly, dressed to the nines and perfectly coifed for the affair. On the other side was a woman in her fifties with black wavy hair and a smooth dark complexion. Earlier I'd noticed her helping the older woman to her chair and getting her food, and now she smiled and welcomed me in a beautifully accented voice. English was clearly not her first language, but she chatted with charming confidence as we settled into our lunch.

I introduced myself, then listened as the elderly woman told me her name and her relationship to the bride and groom. I turned to the other woman and said, "And you must be . . ." I paused for a split second as I searched for the right word: "her nurse" or "companion" or . . . Thankfully she jumped in enthusiastically to fill in the blank.

"I'm Mrs. Watson's friend Esmee!" she said, then told me about her job, not as a paid caregiver but as the CEO of a successful software company. She'd just flown in from a Hawaiian vacation for the wedding, before she was off to a corporate meeting in New York later in the day.

Instantly I realized I'd fallen into an *unconscious bias* that dictated an assumption about Esmee. It made me ignore all the *actual* evidence to the contrary: Every action she'd taken was one of being an attentive friend, not a nurse. Her demeanor was confident, commanding. Her appearance, glamorous. And yet my mind made an instant assumption because of embedded connections in my brain about skin color, long before I was even conscious of them. It was humbling to be reminded of just how far I still needed to grow as a human being.

The lesson here? Don't make snap assumptions. Learn to recognize unconscious bias in your views about people. Realize that we humans are mentally wired to trust those who "look like us" and predisposed to be suspicious of the "other." This leads to mistrust and hostility, hatred and fear. When we reduce people to a caricature based on race, class, accent, gender, career, or age, we shrink our world into who is "in" and who is "out"; who can make valuable contributions and who can be ignored; who is worthy of power and prestige and who should be marginalized; who is worthy of becoming a real boy and who must be sent to the mines. We cheat others of the opportunity to live free and fulfilling lives, and we shortchange ourselves by becoming small-minded and closed.

Dig Deeper

★ Why not take the time to examine your assumptions about people and people groups? What things (stories, literature, family patterns, cultural norms) contribute to your own unconscious bias?

_____

_____

_____

_____

_____

_____

★ What would the world look like if there were no assumptions made about others?

_____

_____

_____

_____

_____

_____

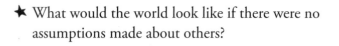

★ When will you let go of false assumptions about someone you work with? Live near? Encounter in your daily life? What would that look like?

_____

_____

_____

_____

_____

_____

NEVER ASSUME

Assumptions about yourself can keep you stuck.

"I'm just a donkey; I can't compete."

"I blew that business decision, so I'm a failure."

"The gatekeepers will say no to my ideas."

"I don't have what it takes to be a _____."

"I'm too old to go back to school."

We all have mental soundtracks that accompany our personal lives, scripted thoughts that seem to follow us along during our important decisions, our everyday moments, and our future plans. Many of those soundtracks function as limiting beliefs that we have placed on ourselves through unconscious connections.

"I failed. I don't deserve another chance."

"A parent abandoned me so I must be unlovable."

"I've picked bad partners in the past. I will never find love."

"I'm not good at numbers, so I can't run a business."

Perhaps you didn't intentionally *decide* to think this way, but somehow these ideas went from fleeting thoughts to ones that seemed to make a lot of sense. Maybe they came from things you heard as a child growing up or from the culture around you, and now they have become habits that are hard to shake. *Here I go again*, you think. *I cannot ever become the person I want to be.*

You are making assumptions about yourself in much the same way a movie director chooses to portray a boy who made a few bad choices: He's a donkey now, and there's nothing that can be done, short of magic. The director plays on the mental connections that will naturally be made by the audience to label the character and project his future. This is similar to the way our brains create a false self-assumption and then find "evidence" to prove that assumption.

"A donkey will never amount to anything good."

What labels are you using for yourself? Are those labels based on an experience that caused you shame? One that created a connection that became hardwired in your mind? Self-labeling generates assumptions that can be hard to dismantle once your brain has decided to make it a "fact." Your brain begins to find evidence to support the assumption.

One simple way to determine whether you have false assumptions about yourself is to fill in the following blanks:

I'm just a _____.
I don't deserve _____.
I'm too old to start _____.

And

I'm only good at _____.
I will achieve _____.
I deserve _____.

What I've found to be true in my own life is that the assumptions I made about myself turned out to be *self-fulfilling*, rather than true assessments of what is possible. I once believed that being a stay-at-home mom was my only calling in life. I loved my role and saw no reason to expand my sights beyond my children and home. Back then I didn't have a model for *what was possible*, and so I assumed that this endeavor would last a lifetime. As my kids got older and life required me to step outside that role and bring in extra income, that assumption caused me distress. I could only think of my newfound creative career as "temporary," rather than worth investing in. It took many years to recognize that the gifts I'd buried, assuming they were unworthy, were actually part of my life calling.

Sometimes assumptions about yourself can keep you from your best work. When Michelangelo was asked by Pope Julius II to paint the Sistine Chapel ceiling, he initially refused because he considered himself to be a sculptor. "I am not in the right place—I am not a painter," he said in a letter to his friend Giovanni da Pistoia. Michelangelo viewed his work as an extension of how he saw himself—an artist who worked in marble, not fresco. How much we would have missed out on if he had limited his work to his own self-assumptions! By agreeing to take on the project, he spent the next four years creating a masterpiece for the ages.

Never assume the thoughts you think about yourself are true. Taking time to replace your false self-perceptions with what's really true will free you to embark on your life's long-term calling and adventure.

Dig Deeper

★ Why not list the limiting assumptions you've made about yourself? Dig deeper to find if these assumptions are based on reality or on faulty foundations. Write what you discover here.

_____

_____

_____

_____

_____

_____

★ What would it look like to leave those limiting assumptions behind? What would it look like to assume that you are creative, inventive, resourceful, able, and whole?

_____

_____

_____

_____

_____

_____

★ When will you decide to change your self-narrative? Date: _____

ALWAYS

Assume the very best of everyone (including yourself) to create freedom, trust, and community.

Changing our snap assumptions—those unconscious biases—is only half of the equation to overcome the obstacles we put in our own way. The second half requires empathetic soul-work in order to fully blossom into the kind of whole-hearted life we wish for—one that is free to explore a boundless world.

Creating new neural pathways is like chopping through dense undergrowth to make a trail. A few years ago, my husband, Tom, decided to make a path through the forested creek area that fills part of our property. He knew I wanted to take my donkeys Flash and Henry on longer and more interesting walks than we had available in the pasture. The initial work was very hard: cutting trees and branches, pulling up roots, and dealing with poison ivy. Once the new trail was cut in, it became possible to take a walk through the previously impenetrable area, but it still required wearing long sleeves and hiking boots to keep from getting poison ivy and being scratched by vines. The trail required more maintenance and grooming beyond the initial cutting to get it—and keep it—in working order. Now, the more our feet (and hooves) have pounded the dirt floor of the path, fewer vines and weeds appear. And now that we don't hit our heads on low-hanging branches, we can even jog through the forest. It has become one of Flash's and Henry's favorite things to do—walk (and trot!) through the trails with eager abandon.

The more the trail is traveled, the easier it becomes to follow it. The same is true for the kinds of empathetic pathways we want our brain's neurons to use. The more we actively create freeways for positive thought patterns, the more easily those thoughts can move into our present realities.

We work to chop out the old, false assumptions about ourselves and others by first recognizing that they exist as a result of our absorption of cultural and familial experiences and attitudes. We then groom and maintain healthy pathways through activities that nurture empathy for others and compassion for ourselves.

What does this kind of empathy and compassion look like? Assume:

- That you could be wrong.
- That everyone is trying their best.
- That you don't know all the answers.
- The best about others.
- That you can learn something from every situation or person you encounter.

But don't stop there. Assume:

- That your potential is unlimited.
- That those who have hurt and disappointed you were hurt and disappointed by others.
- That you can grow your capacity to love and be loved.
- That everyone, if given the same opportunities and love, would be contributing members of society.

In the end, it wasn't wishing upon a star that made Pinocchio become a real boy. He was changed through acts of bravery, honesty, and kindness. It takes all three to let go of assumptions that keep us stuck so we can embrace the positive assumptions that help us grow.

Dig Deeper

★ Why not chop away the unnecessary vines and beliefs that choke out your brain's good pathways? Why not create a beautiful pathway forward by actively maintaining and grooming the trails? Make a list of assumptions that you want to chop out and replace them with positive ones.

_____

_____

_____

★ What would your life look like if you maintained positive assumptions about yourself? What if you assumed you could do "that thing" you always wanted to do? What if you assumed that people would like to help you accomplish it? What would it feel like to assume the best of everyone you encounter? Take the time to describe it.

_____

_____

_____

_____

_____

_____

★ When will you begin to create new assumptions that fill your soul with empathy and compassion? Write that date here: _____

CHAPTER 5

ASSERT

In the ancient Middle East, a celebrity magician named Balaam is in a rage. His donkey Tahira (my name for her) is embarrassing him by refusing to take another step. In fact, she just decided to *lie down* underneath him, much to the amusement of his prestigious traveling companions, who try to hide their snorts of laughter. As a renowned seer of his time, Balaam is accustomed to being courted by powerful people in order to announce prophecies or render blessings or curses on whomever they wish . . . for a price, of course. Visions of fame and fortune make him eager to reach the king of a nearby country who has summoned him. This expedition promises to *really* put him on the map as the premier diviner of his time.

If only his donkey would cooperate.

The hot winds of the landscape swirl around the hills near the Euphrates River and settle like a dead weight over the path of Balaam and his donkey.

This wretched donkey is humiliating me. Tahira's ears are back and she begins to bray, which only makes Balaam angrier.

"I've had it with you!" Balaam grabs his stick and swings it over his head. "This is the third time you've refused to go. First, you run off into a field, then you crush my foot against a wall, and now this?" He begins to beat her with such force he doesn't even notice when Tahira's brays become a comprehensible voice.

She speaks her words distinctly—and clearly, she is *not* happy. "Why are you beating me?"

"Because you've made a fool of me!" Balaam spits through gritted teeth. He glances at the two princes accompanying him, who are now laughing out loud.

"Am I not the donkey you've ridden all your life? Am I in the habit of doing this to you?" Tahira reproaches him with a reminder of her faithful service, her brown eyes imploring him to calm down.

Balaam clears his throat, as if realizing that he is engaged in conversation, uh . . . with his donkey. *Why is she making so much sense right now?* Suddenly something else captures his attention: Balaam can now see exactly *what* made Tahira stop: A sword-brandishing angel stands directly in their path! The donkey hasn't been obstinate; quite the contrary. She has most certainly saved his life. Balaam's face begins to flush an even deeper shade of red.

Now it is the angel's turn to speak. "Why have you beaten your donkey these three times? She's the one with clear vision who saw me and turned away. If she hadn't turned away I would have killed *you* and spared *her*!"

I've often wondered why this strange story is included in ancient biblical Scripture. True, the account ends on a positive note with a blessing pronounced over "the good guys," but all the details leading up to it seem so odd.

Or are they?

You see, the only one who displays any *real* character in this narrative is the donkey, Tahira. Always cast in support roles, never given any speaking lines, donkeys are ever-present in texts like this one but somehow never get listed in the credits. It's safe to say that without those unnamed donkeys, the nomadic journeys of so many people in that time and place in the world would not have been possible . . . and then where would the stories be? But here, Tahira is a standout, a showstopper. While the point of the story may have been the blessing that Balaam gave in spite of being paid handsomely to utter a curse over the Israelite people, it still doesn't answer the question as to why such a comedic lead-in made the final manuscript.

I believe Tahira provides a valuable lesson for those who

are willing to dig a little deeper. Her story shows us that deep insight often arrives through unexpected means, that integrity is revealed in our actions, and that communicating effectively means speaking the language of the listener.

This brave little donkey is forever famous for owning her leadership skills in the midst of a confusing situation. Though she entered the story as a mere humble servant, she changed the whole trajectory of the narrative by asserting her vision, her values, and her voice.

YOUR VISION

Assert a clear vision for the future you want to create.

As a donkey your eyes are uniquely positioned so you can see not only what's in front of you, but what's behind you as well. Unlike most creatures that have limited views, the donkey's 360-degree perspective provides you with your own superpower: the ability to assert a vision for the future while acknowledging what's all around.

Those who flourish in their work do so because they have clarity of vision. They can see what others cannot. They are able to see beyond the here and now to a future that offers a path forward to those who follow. Embracing your inner donkey means you can be a visionary leader.

To become this kind of leader, you'll need to draw upon unexpected sources. It's your 360-degree view that sees the past and present as foundational pieces in the quest to create your vision. It's all about owning your story, and it begins by asking yourself (and answering) these key questions:

- What recurring themes have been present in my journey?
- What lessons have I learned along the way?
- What things have worked for me in the past?
- What things haven't worked?
- How did I get to where I am today?

Asking questions like these while formulating a vision for the future provides a sturdy framework to build upon. They bring clarity to the present and initiate motivation—the "why"—that makes your plan sustainable. A visionary is a creative thinker who is willing to tug on the threads of personal and collective history to design aspirations that are bigger than what was believed possible. That design becomes a tapestry of meaningful work and a shared commitment with your herd, which we'll talk about in the next chapter.

In their book *The Leadership Challenge*, James Kouzes and Barry Posner state, "Envisioning the future is not about gazing into a fortune-teller's crystal ball; it's about paying attention to the little things that are going on all around you and being able to recognize patterns that point to the future."

Being a visionary is one of the most important qualities you can have as a change-maker or leader. A leader's vision for the future of their organization, whether it's a Fortune 500 company or a family, is only as valuable as it is relatable to the team he or she is leading. In other words, *the vision must be attached to the shared history and values* of the people it hopes to inspire, in just the same way that your personal vision is attached to your own story and values. You see, the need for developing a clear vision isn't just for CEOs; it's for everyone who wants to create a lasting legacy through their work or passion.

In my own career as a solopreneur, I had to be nimble enough to respond to my clients' needs by continually inventing and reinventing my work. Each art commission required me to mine my own resources and creativity to make something beautiful or create a solution for a design problem. The same was true for writing books and creating online content. I was good at defining felt needs and coming up with ideas to address them, but I was less effective as a team member when projects required collaboration.

As I began to redirect my efforts into new areas, I wanted to build upon what had worked for me in the past, find the recurring themes, pay attention to the areas of weakness, and consider who my work serves currently. In order to assert a fresh vision for the next leg of my career as a creative leader, I'd need to pull from all these threads to create my "why." The result? Clarity and focus. Insight to create possibilities and opportunities—not just for myself, but for my herd—those for whom my work is intended.

Assert your vision by owning your 360-degree view. It puts you in a position to create change—and work—that lasts.

Dig Deeper

★ Why not find your "why"? Jot down why you do what you do and clarify why it is important to you. This is a foundational step toward having a lasting vision.

_____

_____

_____

★ What would 360-degree vision look like for you? What would your past self tell your present self about what you need for the future?

_____

_____

_____

★ When will you have a vision-casting meeting with yourself (or your team)?
Date: _____

YOUR VALUES

Your values are expressed by what you habitually do.

Integrity, kindness, loyalty, and humble service are the values that Tahira asserted through her actions. Not just on the fateful day when she saved her master's life, but every day that had preceded it. When she was falsely accused of wrongdoing, she gave an unassailable self-defense because her character—her reputation—was beyond reproach. She was exonerated by her history of living by her values.

When you embrace your inner donkey, you live true to these same core values that make you who you are. True leaders lead by example—by what they do, not just what they say. Asserting your values means that you live your life and create work that is congruent with what you say you believe. This requires a level of risk because it puts your values on public display.

To assert is to get out ahead and lead with conviction. There is a possibility that people will not consider someone who leads with humble service as their North Star. There is a chance that loyalty and kindness may be seen as weakness in your work, that you may be taken advantage of or passed over. However, when your personal work ethic demands that others are treated with respect and empathy, true leadership emerges, and the deep work of your calling can be done. This is foundational to work that lasts for the long haul.

That's the conviction of Robert Chesnut, the former chief ethics officer for Airbnb and author of *Intentional Integrity: How Smart Companies Can Lead an Ethical Revolution*: "Leaders must openly and directly talk about integrity, embrace it as part of the culture, and be ready to do the 'right thing,' even if it appears to hurt business in the short run." In his leadership position with Airbnb, he led a weekly interactive orientation for new employees to talk specifically about ethical issues that might arise and how to handle them. Being clear and up-front about how you approach sticky situations with integrity gives employees, followers, and customers confidence that they can trust your leadership, product, or service.

A starting place to ascertain what values you live by is to simply ask, "What does my reputation say about me?" Does it say that you are driven, ruthless, and demanding? Does it say that you meet or exceed your customer's expectations? That you work with diligence and pay attention to the needs and well-being of others? Does it say that you value integrity and doing things right, or that you are willing to cut corners and leverage people to attain your goal?

Asserting the values you live by means that you never have to worry about damage control for doing something unethical. If you ever find yourself concerned about covering your tracks to avoid scrutiny or liability, you'll know that you've compromised your own integrity and need to go back and make things right. It calls for humility and a willingness to change course to get back on track.

Fortunately for donkeys, your values stand the test of time and create a path forward that's worthy of being followed.

Dig Deeper

★ Why not be clear about your values as an individual (or as a company)? How does being vague about your values compromise your ability to lead others with conviction? Take time to write those values out.

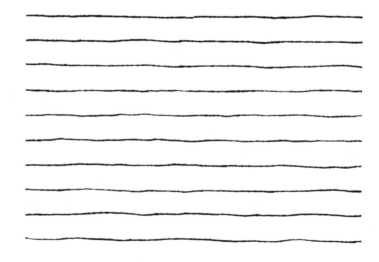

★ What would it take to create an environment that reflects integrity? What would it take to go from "legal but unethical" as an operating standard to a values-directed standard?

_____

_____

_____

_____

_____

_____

_____

_____

_____

_____

★ When will you actively pursue integrity as a core value? Put a date on the calendar to create ethical guidelines, based on your values, for your life and work.

Date: _____

YOUR VOICE

Be proud of what makes your voice unique.

Your voice is distinctively yours, and this world needs you to assert it.

No one sounds exactly like you. Your voice is the thing that makes your message powerful and your work impactful. Your unique voice is best understood by your herd—your people.

Given the right conditions, a donkey's peculiar bray can be heard fifty miles away or even farther. Now *that's* impressive projection! It's a call that communicates presence to all other donkeys in the area, alerts them to danger, and even expresses loneliness. To our human ears, all "hee-haws" sound the same, but in reality, each individual donkey has its own sound and resonance that is heard and understood at a level we cannot comprehend.

Going back to our story about Tahira, she had tried every which way to communicate to Balaam the danger she saw ahead, but until she spoke in a manner that *he* could distinguish, her message just couldn't break through. She had asserted her vision and her values, but she needed her voice to make it abundantly clear. She needed to use the language of her listener to get her point across.

Asserting your voice takes courage. It means you risk being

misunderstood, but you do it anyway because your message is too important to leave to chance.

HEE-HAW, HEE-HAW, HEE-HAW! (Go ahead, I dare you to try it!)

As humans we may laugh at a donkey's bray, but then we are reminded that a donkey isn't speaking to *us*. A donkey is communicating to her own audience, in the way her audience understands best. Her bray sounds like music to their long ears. It's what they've been waiting for! It resonates and reverberates because it's for *them*. It's helpful to realize this when we create our work, or craft our message, or lead our team. Asserting your authentic voice means that your message *lands* with your herd—often at a deep level of understanding—because they *get* you, and they know that you get them.

But that doesn't always happen on its own.

A friend of mine once told me about a time that she received a birthday gift from a college student from another country whom she had helped get settled in the United States. The student arrived at the party bearing an elaborately wrapped present topped with a huge handmade bow—it was almost like a work of art. My friend was so wowed by the package that she couldn't wait to see what was inside! *It must be something extraordinary*, she thought. She tore into the package and found an elegant box which contained the gift artfully laid between layers of tissue. It was a plastic fly swatter. She was speechless. Was this a joke?

Should she laugh? She looked at her friend, who seemed just as confused by the way she'd torn the beautiful paper wrapping. "Thank you so much! How thoughtful," she managed to say.

It was not until much later she learned that in her student's culture, the gift was all about the *presentation*, not the actual item being given. What was meaningful was the *way* it was wrapped, the care that was taken. Suddenly my friend could see all the love and thoughtfulness that went into that gift, and it made a difference when it came time to reciprocate. When it was her student's birthday, she took time to wrap her gift beautifully so that she would be sure to receive the message of love that went into it. They finally understood one another.

How you communicate your message matters. Whether through the spoken or written word, through work that you create, or through branding and advertising, it's the vehicle that represents you and your work to the world. When the "how" and the "what" line up, your message hits the sweet spot of your intended audience, customer, or coworker—and this rarely happens by chance. For most of us, it takes time spent listening, observing, and being a student of our audience to find out what they need and want. And it takes commitment to discover our own authentic voice—the values and beliefs that animate our story, art, service, or presence we offer.

Trust that your authentic voice is what your people—those in your herd—need to hear.

Dig Deeper

★ Why not ask yourself what your authentic voice sounds like? What is your main message? Write it here.

———————————————
———————————————
———————————————
———————————————
———————————————

★ What would it look like to assert your authentic voice? How would it change your message?

———————————————
———————————————
———————————————
———————————————

★ When will you write an email, blog post, article, or book using your authentic voice? When will you make that phone call, schedule that meeting, or agree to speak to a group?
Date: _____

LEAN IN TO YOUR UNIQUE STRENGTHS

CHAPTER 6

ASSEMBLE

In the desert of the American Southwest, a young burro named Zuni presses into her mother's side. Their small herd of wild donkeys pauses at the top of the canyon wall. Below them, down a steep descent and into the ravine through a thick growth of cacti and sagebrush is the hidden spring. Siba, Zuni's mother, is the group's matriarch who stands in the lead. She raises her nose, lifting her upper lip as she inhales the air for signs of danger. Mountain lions have been on the prowl all summer, waiting for their opportunity to pick off the oldest and weakest donkeys in the close-knit band of eight.

Siba glances over her shoulder at two young jacks and signals for them to begin the descent, motioning with her ears for them to take the narrow path. Five-month-old Zuni tries to grab one last gulp of her mother's milk, but Siba noses her away and turns her toward the line of donkeys awaiting their turn to go.

I'll be right behind you, Siba communicates, sensing Zuni's nervousness. She nibbles Zuni's tail, hoping to tease her into calming down. Zuni has never felt such a cloud of fear over her extended family and friends as she does just now, but her mother's playfulness has the intended effect. She shakes her oversized ears and spins in a circle, catching a glimpse of her father in the distance, ready to leap into action in case of attack. His notched ears and scarred neck are a testament to the fierce battles he's already fought against mountain lions, coyotes, and other male burros trying to subvert his dominance. Zuni squares her shoulders and tries to look as regal as her hero.

The eight donkeys make their way down the steep canyon path in search of the spring on the valley floor, hidden not only by brush, but under twelve inches of dirt. Able to go several days without water, the burros have a "sixth sense" that guides them to underground sources. Zuni watches as Siba and the others put their noses to the ground and begin to zero in on their target like diviners. Taking a cue from her elders, Zuni mimics their movements although she doesn't quite know what smell she should be searching for. She finds herself following the scent of a rabbit instead, her long legs zigzagging around a cactus and getting tangled up in the process. Caught off balance, Zuni does a face-plant, bottom up, her mouth filling with dust.

Suddenly the others stop at a spot in the dry riverbed and begin to paw at the ground. Zuni's head pops up from behind the sagebrush where the rabbit disappeared, her ears tipped forward in excitement. They found something! Spitting dirt and tripping over her own feet, Zuni gallops back to the herd that is intently digging in the sand with their hooves. The sand gives way to mud, and finally to precious water bubbling up from below. Siba nudges Zuni forward to the water hole and keeps watch while she drinks the cool liquid. She knows that once the herd finishes, other desert animals will be drawn to this uncovered treasure, alerted by the chirping of the birds who will arrive first. Soon there will be a creature party here lasting for days on end.

Zuni's little herd met the challenge and hardship of the high desert through their communal efforts. Each one participated to protect the herd and help it flourish in an inhospitable environment. Without the support of a herd, a lone donkey in the desert faces certain danger. Each individual is made stronger by the social bonds of the burro community. For their efforts, they supply water to the greater community of animals around them.

When you want to create lasting change, not only in your personal life but in the larger world, you, too, need a community. Whether that looks like starting a business, raising a family, leading a company, making art, or serving others, embracing your own inner donkey means leaning in to your unique gifts and strengths—but it doesn't stop there. It also acknowledges that it "takes a village" to do meaningful work that has impact for the long haul. You can't go it alone. In fact, in order to do the work you're meant for, you'll need others who are willing to come alongside you to lean in as well. You need people who resonate with and amplify your message, and still others who can provide mentorship for you as you put your ideas into the universe. Being part of a community of like-minded creators, entrepreneurs, or leaders makes your work better and more powerful than it could ever be as a solo operation.

What does this mean for you? It means you'll need to assemble that team: your heroes, your helpers, and your herd.

YOUR HEROES

Who you look up to says everything about who you will become.

Everyone has at least one hero. Someone to admire, study, and emulate; someone who has become an example to follow. Zuni has the influence of her mother and her father to follow; leaders who are fearless in the face of danger, ones who let the other donkeys in the herd partake of the water first while they keep watch. Her father has earned his position by chasing off any other male burro who might try to challenge him and assert his dominance over the younger males already in the herd. But it is her mother, Siba, who keeps the tribe together and makes decisions for their daily well-being. There is a language of leadership with the group—understood at a molecular level through eons of time and instinctive communication. The leader must earn the respect of the herd through the means that donkeys understand.

Hopefully, our heroes are not going to have *literal* fights with others to claim their position, but they will have fought other kinds of battles to earn a level of noble achievement, or notable courage against the odds. Who our heroes are says a lot about the kind of people we want to become. If they exhibit character under pressure, personal integrity when it would be easy to be unethical, and leadership in times of crisis, we know we are following someone worthy of our trust. Heroes who have achieved the kind of success in the arenas we want to be part of have a special place of honor in our lives.

So who are your heroes? In a celebrity-driven culture like ours, it's easy to mistake fame for hero status. Social media influencers, television personalities, and movie stars are imitated for what they wear, promote, and project as images of themselves. Maybe they are, in fact, who they seem to be, but being internet famous is not the same as being a hero-quality leader. The good news is, in this world, you get to choose the leaders who exemplify the values you aspire to, those who inspire you to become a better version of yourself.

Heroes can be found in the pages of history or may be current leaders in your industry or sphere—people whom you don't know personally. There is much you can glean from these individuals through articles, interviews, and books. Even better is to find a mentor who can personally invest their time and share their expertise with you, just as George Washington invested in Alexander Hamilton by mentoring him during the Revolutionary War and later appointing Hamilton to the president's Cabinet as secretary of the treasury. I have personally had the pleasure of mentoring other artists, writers, and young parents who have reached out for advice and guidance.

Mentoring can take place in coffee shops, on factory floors, and in conference rooms and living rooms. Establish a relationship with someone (that is, on their terms) who is further ahead of you in experience. Their wealth of knowledge and confidence will be assets as you move forward in your journey.

Assemble your heroes. Find people who are doing the kind of good work you want to do in this world, and study their leadership style. How are they serving others with their skills and expertise? What can you learn from their stories of overcoming difficulties? What values do they possess that you can internalize for yourself?

Your heroes determine the trajectory of your story.

Dig Deeper

★ Why not identify one or more individuals you admire, and write down the qualities they inspire in you?

_____

_____

_____

_____

★ What would it look like if you had a chance to meet and talk with your hero? Based on what you know about them, what advice would they likely give you?

_____

_____

_____

_____

★ When will you set up a time to meet personally with someone you admire?
Date: _____

YOUR HELPERS

Long-haul success is achieved only with a team of contributors.

The best way to find your helpers is to *be* a helper.

In chapter 3, we looked at the significance of ascribing honor to those who have helped us get to where we are now. And yet we sometimes forget the importance of assembling the same caliber of helpers for the *new* successes we dream of in the future. Somehow, we feel we must forge ahead on our own, rather than taking lessons from our past.

Assembling your helpers means actively seeking out those individuals who can assist you with advice, resources, encouragement, and connections. It means finding people in your field and out of it. These aren't necessarily heroes, but are simply people with whom you are intentionally creating a friendly relationship.

This endeavor is not a one-way street. The best helping relationships are communal in nature, mutually beneficial to one another. You cannot simply be a taker; you must seek to be a giver. In fact, the starting place for this kind of relationship is to become generous with your *own* advice, resources, encouragement, and connections.

In business terms, this is often called "networking," something that *can* feel a little smarmy and uncomfortable. I suspect few people really enjoy going to after-hours meetups to pass out their business cards and try to schmooze their way onto some important person's dinner guest list. And doing favors for the express purpose of getting a favor in return isn't a good basis for a genuine relationship. That feels icky because it *is* icky.

When you embrace a long-haul approach to doing work that is meaningful, you stop valuing people only for what they can do for you. Instead, you step into an ethos of generosity, a way of living that is all about connecting with others, providing value, and finding ways to contribute. You will naturally find people who will reciprocate—not because they owe you something but as an outgrowth of warmth and goodwill. It's called "being a friend." When you look out for the needs of others and seek out ways to help *them* succeed, *that is an end in itself.* Living generously means taking the time to learn what someone is interested in, what they love, and how they want to make their own impact. You'll experience a special kind of joy when you contribute to their work or to their personal lives. Eventually, in the way of the universe, that kind of action always comes back to you in some way, shape, or form.

My friend Bridgette, an architectural designer, is a great example of this. She loves her small town, so several years ago she joined a volunteer civic organization that meets weekly to discuss the needs of the community. She's built caring relationships with the other members through their shared concerns and interests. When one of those members knew of a non-profit organization that was looking for someone to design a new facility, naturally she recommended Bridgette for the project. That project—a resource center for underserved people in the community—became a two-year source of income for Bridgette, and even better, it was aligned with her values.

Expand your circle of business associates, friends, coworkers, and professional groups *before* you need anything from anyone—not *because* you need something. Get involved with volunteer organizations, hobbies, or activities you enjoy and get to know other like-minded people. When you enlarge your relationships through kind interest and helpful interactions, you'll find a team of helpers ready to reciprocate down the road.

Dig Deeper

★ Why not join a group that shares your interests? What are you keenly enthusiastic about? Do you love cats, or Dodgers baseball, or hiking? Don't limit your networking to workplace events or people.

_____

_____

_____

_____

★ What would it look like to give generously of your time and expertise to someone who cannot reciprocate in kind? What would be the downside to volunteering with an organization in your area of interest? What would be the upside?

_____

_____

_____

_____

_____

_____

_____

_____

_____

_____

_____

★ When will you schedule coffee with someone you'd like to know better? Write that date here: _____

YOUR HERD

Your people are the ones who resonate with you, your message, and your work.

Your herd is made up of the people your work serves. These are the ones who "get" your message and your whole self, through shared experiences, shared goals, and shared community. These are the recipients of your best work, creativity, and generosity.

You see, you cannot serve everyone all the time. To try would be a waste of energy and resources. Not everyone wants or needs what you have to offer, and that's okay. But there are others who are just waiting and hoping for the kind of work that only you can do. Maybe it's your art, or your writing, or your research, or your specific talent that they are looking for. These are the people to seek out and serve.

The same is true with whatever you create: When you realize *who* it is that your work serves, everything changes. Work for them, for their betterment, for their success. Your herd, in turn, supports you—and your success. When your work lands in the right place, with the right herd, your capacity for creative growth and impact on others is exponential. Your herd will trust your leadership and your contribution because they connect with you on a deeper level.

Kristin Schell was a busy mom of four who dreamed of a slower pace of life that had room for connection with other people—like the kind of lifestyle she'd experienced as a student living abroad in France. She loved how people there lingered over meals, creating time for conversation and relationships, and she wished there was a way to bring that back home to the United States. Between kids, activities, work schedules, and responsibilities, life didn't offer much opportunity for what she was craving.

One day, desperate for a way to slow down and connect, she put a simple wooden picnic table in her front yard, painted it turquoise, and invited friends and neighbors to join her. As a result, not only did life change in her small community, but what started as *one* Turquoise Table became an entire movement of people who wanted to experience something similar. Turquoise Tables can now be found in all fifty states and in countries around the world, places where neighbors and friends can slow down and gather together. A simple invitation to sit and chat in the front yard began a ripple effect of connection and joy.

Kristin found her people—her herd—by paying attention to her own story and leaning in to the things she valued. When she shared her passion for creating community, people who were looking for a message like hers responded. They resonated with her message of hospitality and became a self-designated community of "Front Yard People."

Now, it takes time and effort to be able to define who your

work is for. Sometimes you're not sure what your work should even *be*, so how can you find an audience when you don't know what the message is? Go back to your story, the one we talked about in "Own Your Story." Revisit your past and present. Challenge your assumptions and refine your vision. Continue to "Give Yourself Permission" to ask questions and have aspirations to do your truest, bravest, and goodest work.

When you add value where you can by seeking ways to serve others, eventually everything will come into focus. You will find your herd when the beautiful fusion of your story and work is launched consistently into the world.

Our little Zuni is a lucky burro. She is learning early on the power of assembling her team: her heroes, her helpers, and her herd. She has firsthand experience seeing how working together toward a common goal creates a positive ecosphere that ripples into the wider world.

Dig Deeper

★ Why not spend time identifying your herd? Who does your work benefit? Who resonates with your message? Why not revisit your own story for clues?

_____

_____

_____

★ What would it look like to have your message land with people who love and appreciate what you have to offer? How would it change your idea of serving if you were to narrow your focus?

_____

_____

_____

_____

_____

★ What are some effective ways you can serve your herd? Jot down your ideas.

_____

_____

_____

_____

_____

★ Then decide the target date when you will put things into action. Date: _____

CHAPTER 7

ASSETS

"Ah, Susumaniello!" The wizened vineyard keeper chuckles and then leans closer. "This is a very special grape." He adjusts his hat and rests his arm on his shovel as he looks across the landscape to the shimmering Adriatic Sea in the distance. This vineyard has been tended by his family for generations, and he knows every kind of grape that's grown on the arid slopes of southern Italy's Salento peninsula.

"We call this grape 'the little donkey.'" He laughs out loud. "Little black donkey!" He still remembers when grape harvests were loaded onto donkeys that carried them from the vineyards to the wineries.

In this southernmost Puglia region known for its enchanting scenic hills and beautiful wine-making traditions, this rare ancient grape has been rediscovered and brought into its own spotlight. Found only on a few acres of the country, the small black grapes were once difficult to identify and locate within larger plantings of other types of vines.

You see, in the early twentieth century the donkey grape fell out of favor as winemakers in the region preferred other varieties that could easily produce greater quantities of wine. Gradually, the Susumaniello was replaced, and the only remaining plantings were tucked in corners and on rugged hillsides where little else would grow.

Mark Shannon, the winemaker who is credited with rediscovering the beautiful assets of this grape, admits this kind of grape is tricky to work with. He says, "It is resilient, reliable and obstinate—with a heart of gold," adding, "It is relatively easy to grow, but not necessarily to the specification a winemaker might seek—and it is not at all easy to vinify. It is very 'donkey-like' in that regard as well." Mark must identify and select the grapes from the individual family vineyards, and then treat them to a special process that makes the most of their unique properties.

Resilient enough to withstand harsh conditions, they seem to flourish in sandy soils without the irrigation most plantings need. With a resourceful use of energy, their compact vines produce extremely heavy clusters of grapes, which the old-timers say is the reason the grape received its affectionate name "little donkey." It's a nod to the donkeys that have been used in the vineyards for centuries as pack animals that are able to carry baskets loaded high with grapes. Perhaps it is also because of the fruit's stubborn nature, in not responding to the wine processes as expected, that the name stuck. No one really knows for sure, but the description is fitting.

Once overlooked and underappreciated, the Susumaniello was considered useful only as a "helping" grape, providing volume and flavor to other wines. But its classic qualities are the very things that have helped it survive and now thrive with a newfound respect. There is a lesson here for us: All too often in our race to get ahead in life, we overlook our own best assets by choosing quantity over quality. We make the mistake of placing highest value on things like talent, academic achievement, and personal style. But the truth is that our most valuable assets run far deeper and provide a more solid path toward a meaningful life.

It takes resilience to thrive in difficult circumstances, like the donkey grape that clings to rocky, windswept hillsides near the sea. Where others look for easy growth, resilient people like you find their roots growing deep and developing strength through the challenges they face. It takes a special kind of resourcefulness to discover opportunities in unlikely places. Perhaps what works for others won't work for you. You've developed a knack for seeing possibilities where others see none. Finally, staying the course toward your vision requires a level of donkey stubbornness, which we will affectionately call "resolve." You've got grit . . . with a kick.

RESILIENT

You are able to bounce back from adversity and disappointment.

If you're a donkey, you are *made* to thrive in difficult conditions.

As a desert animal, you are built for rocky terrain and hot sun. You are able to travel arduous paths and endure hardships because of your inner strength and resilience. In fact, one of your best qualities is your ability to get back up after you've been knocked down.

There is an old tale about a donkey. Harvey Mackay tells it best:

Once upon a time, a young donkey asked his grandpa, "How do I grow up to be just like you?"

"Oh, that's simple," the elder donkey said. "All you have to do is remember to shake it off and step up."

"What does that mean?" asked the youngster.

The grandfather replied, "Let me tell you a story. . . . Once, when I was your age, I was out walking. I wasn't paying attention and fell deep into an old abandoned well. I started braying and braying. Finally an old farmer came by and saw me. I was scared to death. But then he left. I stayed in that well all night.

"The next morning, he came back with a whole group of people, and they looked down at me. Then the old farmer said, 'The well is abandoned and that donkey isn't worth saving, so let's get to work.' And believe it or not, they started to shovel dirt into the well. I was going to be buried alive!

"After the first shovels of dirt came down on me, I realized something. Every time dirt landed on my back, I could shake it off and use it to step up a bit higher! They kept shoveling, and I kept shaking the dirt off and stepping up.

"'Shake it off and step up . . . shake it off and step up . . .' I kept repeating to myself for encouragement. And it wasn't long before I stepped out of the well, exhausted but triumphant.

"So no matter how difficult the situation . . . no matter how bad things get . . . no matter how much dirt gets dumped on you, just remember—shake it off and step up. You'll be all right."

Everyone encounters hard situations and setbacks, but those who embrace their inner donkeys become adept at finding a way up and through hard times. When you choose to outlast and outwit difficulties, you increase your ability to grow in your own resilience, which in turn helps you succeed in the long run. Resilience helps you see each challenge you face as a learning opportunity, an emotional muscle that is strengthened with practice.

"It's not what happens to you, but how you handle what happens to you, that's going to make the difference" Zig Ziglar often said. Someone who personifies this is Mallory Weggemann, a young woman who became paralyzed from the waist down following a routine medical procedure in 2008. Mallory had been a competitive swimmer, but this dramatic change in her life didn't stop her from doing what she loved. It took her less than two years to claim eight world records. Going into the 2012 Summer Paralympic Games in London, she held fifteen world records and thirty-four American records, and added gold and bronze medals there. Then she went on to win two golds and a silver at the 2019 World Para Swimming Championships, even after a fall that severely damaged her left arm.

Perhaps most of us will not become Olympians following an injury, but we do have everyday situations where we can tap into our own resilience by refusing to let adversity keep us down. My daughter Lauren's resilience was tested when several doctors tried to convince her that her concern for feeling "off" was all in her head. She kept going to other doctors until she finally found one willing to do further testing, resulting in a diagnosis of postural orthostatic tachycardia syndrome (POTS), a blood circulation disorder. After receiving the right treatment, Lauren bounced back into a life that's filled with her family and meaningful work.

Resilience can be developed over time in big and small ways. Shake it off and step up.

Dig Deeper

★ Instead of asking, "Why me?" when faced with a difficult setback, can you reframe it as "Why not me?" How does this change your perspective?

_____

_____

_____

_____

_____

_____

_____

★ What would "bouncing back" look like in your current adversity? Describe it.

_____

_____

_____

_____

_____

_____

_____

★ When will you take steps toward bouncing back? Create a timeline.

_____

_____

_____

_____

_____

_____

_____

RESOURCEFUL

You find opportunities and sustenance in overlooked places.

Donkeys are resourceful.

If you're a donkey, you are able to discover what you need in surprising and underappreciated places.

"You'll be fine," the donkey expert told me over the phone. "You've got a safe pasture that's fully fenced and a dry shelter to protect your new donkey from the elements, and you've had him checked out by a vet."

I didn't know a thing about taking care of a donkey, so when Flash showed up on my driveway, I began scouring the internet for help. I found a donkey expert who was willing to take some time to give me a few tips and pointers. During our conversation I felt my confidence grow.

Then the man said something that surprised me: "Just be sure he doesn't eat too much grass."

I had been taking notes as fast as my hand could move but I stopped mid-sentence.

"Wait. Isn't that all a donkey eats?" I asked.

"Well, donkeys are browsers by nature," he said with a laugh. "They love to look for weeds and vines, sticks and bark, and leaves from trees. Unlike other equines, their digestive systems are able to pull nutrients out of stuff that would make a horse turn up his nose. But donkeys run into trouble when there is *too much* grass for them to eat. The high sugar content can make them sick, and even make them go lame."

"I had no idea," I said. I knew then that Flash (and later Henry) would be fine on our scrubby Texas property. There were plenty of weeds and brush for him to find the right kind of sustenance, although I'd have to watch him in the spring, when natural rye grass is abundant. True to form, donkeys are incredibly resourceful in locating just what they need, in the dead of winter or the dog days of summer where we live. I have to laugh when I see both Flash and Henry's bodies practically buried in the thicket, with nothing but their behinds sticking out as they browse for the coveted leaves inside.

Resourcefulness is one of the qualities I love best about donkeys. They are healthiest when they have to find what sustains them in those overlooked places. They do best when they have to work a little bit for their sustenance. They love the challenge of finding the one tasty leaf in a pile of brush. Embracing your inner donkey means that you, too, are suited for challenges in life that require beating some bushes and finding opportunities where you least expect them.

That's what a man named Pat Flynn did. When he was let go from his job as an architect in 2008, he wasn't sure what to do next. No one was hiring during that economic downturn, so he decided to look in an unexpected place for a source of income. He had been publishing a blog that had a modest number of followers, so he used it as a starting point. He offered a downloadable pdf to help people study for professional certification as architects. Within a month, he had so many sales he knew he had created a path forward for himself—and others. Since then, Pat's resourcefulness has led to a variety of multimillion-dollar businesses, and he helps thousands of other people lean in to their own ideas and passions to do the same. He credits the "worst thing" that could have happened to him—losing his job—as the catalyst for finding the best things.

When there are no easy answers to a problem, no readily available resources to meet the need, you can develop a knack for sniffing out creative solutions. Resourceful entrepreneurs dream up business opportunities that others haven't considered. Resourceful managers know how to help their workers create their best work. Resourceful employees find ways to solve problems on their own. Resourceful teachers discover innovative ways to help their students learn, often on a shoestring budget and without much outside support. Resourceful parents figure out how to stretch a dollar to provide for their children. When roadblocks to progress happen, resourceful people learn how to apply effort, think outside the box, and create solutions that get things back on track.

Dig Deeper

★ Why not ask yourself, "What haven't I considered yet? What have I overlooked when trying to solve my problem or situation?" Remind yourself by recording your answers here.

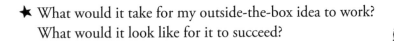

_____

_____

_____

_____

_____

_____

★ What would it take for my outside-the-box idea to work? What would it look like for it to succeed?

_____

_____

_____

_____

_____

_____

_____

★ What deadlines will I set for myself to come up with a new solution? Break it down into steps with separate dates as needed and also a completion date.

_____

_____

_____

_____

_____

_____

RESOLVED

Be stubborn about the things that matter.

It's the quality that donkeys are most famous for: the tenacious grit that digs in and does not give up. We like to call it *resolve.*

May I let you in on a little secret? Donkeys don't really like to be called "stubborn," because that word implies they are being hardheaded, unyielding, and difficult to work with. But there is a flip side of "stubborn" we *do* like: being "fixed or set in purpose or opinion; *resolute.*" This side of stubborn is the side that holds fast to convictions, shows courage in the face of opposition, and stands firm in its purpose. It's a level of grit that simply does not give up on what's worthwhile. Talk about a donkey asset!

Often it's not difficult circumstances or dramatic problems that throw us off course; it's simply the *dailiness* of sticking with something for the long haul that is the true challenge. Day after day, month after month, time and time again, it takes a donkey-brand of stubbornness to see us through the ordinariness. Psychologist Angela Duckworth, a leading researcher, defines this kind of grit as "perseverance and passion for long-term goals," which is associated with continued interest, self-control, and deferring short-term gratification.

Resolve is commitment to long-term goals by developing consistent habits to achieve success. James Clear, author of *Atomic Habits*, says, "Grit isn't about getting an incredible dose of inspiration or courage. It's about building the daily habits that allow you to stick to a schedule and overcome challenges and distractions over and over and over again." It keeps you going, even when you don't feel like getting up and doing that same thing one more time. This kind of stubbornness is the key asset that determines how far you will go, how long you'll last, and how much you'll accomplish.

It takes courage not only to say, "I will try again," but also, "I will keep going." Donkey stubbornness—resolve—commits to doing the work it takes to reach that goal. It is the athlete who gets up at 4:00 a.m. every morning for swim practice; it's the parent who cares for and nurtures their children; it's the couple who works at their forty-year marriage by doing daily kindnesses for one another. When you believe your efforts are meaningful and have value, you find a way to stick with it.

The quote "Opportunity is missed by most people because it is dressed in overalls and looks like hard work" has often been attributed to Thomas Edison, although its origins are disputed. In a culture that prizes fame, making a splash, and being an influencer, resolve seems like an old-fashioned trait. It's not glamorous to put in the time behind the scenes to make something worthwhile happen, but when you embrace your inner donkey, this is what you do best. You aren't afraid to lean in to self-discipline or creating good habits because you know it's like working in a gold mine: You have to be willing to go down deep into the mine—time after time—to bring up the treasure. Most trips will result in loads of worthless rocks being hauled up, but you keep going back because you know there is a mother lode of riches to be discovered.

You are resolved. You have donkey-stubborn grit.

You have what it takes to keep going.

Dig Deeper

★ Why not create a long-term goal that is meaningful to you? What is keeping you from committing to it? Stake your claim on a goal right here:

★ What would it take to reach that goal? Imagine yourself at the completion of your goal and reverse engineer it: What did you do to get there?

★ When will you establish habits that will move you toward your goal? Planning date:

Donkey-stubborn:
a level of grit
that simply does not
give up on
what's worthwhile.

CHAPTER 8

ASTOUND

"If you give a donkey a pancake, he will want some syrup to go with it."

Long before a pig was getting syrup-drenched pancakes in Laura Numeroff's children's book, a pancake-loving donkey charmed the world with his remarkable adventures in the pages of *Brighty of the Grand Canyon*. The book by Marguerite Henry is based on a real-life burro who lived in and around the canyon from about 1882 to 1922—an improbable hero with an unforgettable story and legacy.

One day a wild burro is found sitting in an abandoned miner's camp, as if waiting for someone to return. He is given the name Bright Angel (Brighty for short), after Bright Angel

Creek, and he becomes something of a mascot for the canyon. Never truly tamed, he wanders freely—spending summers on the North Rim with the game warden Jim Owen or with the Thomas McKee family who manages the summer camp and concessions for tourists, offering his services in exchange for snacks and attention. Brighty lets children ride him and hauls water to the camp alongside young Bob McKee, who rewards the donkey with pancakes, but he draws the line for anyone else who tries to use him as a pack animal by scraping their loads off. He uses tree trunks or canyon walls to work the packs from his back and get free of them. He is known to kick a man if he feels he is a dishonest individual, and he cleverly hides in plain sight when he doesn't want to be found. When the cold months arrive, he bids farewell to human companions and spends winters on his own at the bottom of the canyon where it is warmer.

Through his relationship with the game warden and his knowledge of the canyon landscape, Brighty actually helps solve a murder mystery, and is such a local celebrity that he meets Teddy Roosevelt and allegedly even joins the president and his son Quentin on a mountain lion hunt. When the Kaibab Trail Suspension Bridge is built across the Colorado River at the base of the canyon, Brighty is the celebrity who leads the crowd as they cross it during the inaugural ceremony.

Brighty's story comes to life in the pages of the book that Ms. Henry writes, which becomes an instant success in 1953.

Readers everywhere fall in love with this scrappy little burro, and before long the book is turned into a movie, which charms an even *larger* audience. A bronze statue of Brighty is donated to the Grand Canyon's South Rim visitor center, where it becomes a tourist attraction that inspires great interest in the feral burros who still roam the canyon.

Now, this is where Brighty's story takes an unforgettable twist. Turns out, he wasn't done making an impact on the world. By the 1970s there is a push to return the Grand Canyon to its original natural state, culling any animal that is not indigenous to the region. Large numbers of wild donkeys are quietly exterminated. But Little Brighty's statue, his bronze nose rubbed shiny by the thousands of visitors who touch it for good luck, turns into a public flashpoint. The Park puts the statue in storage, hoping people will forget Brighty's story, but they are not prepared for the huge uproar that decision makes. People rally for the return of the statue, but more importantly they become aware of the plight of the wild burros in the canyon. Fundraising efforts pay off, and most of the remaining burros are airlifted from the canyon and rehomed rather than killed. Even more significant, donkey rescue is established as a powerful movement that continues to help these beautiful animals to this day. And Brighty's statue finds a permanent home in the Grand Canyon Lodge on the North Rim.

All because of one astounding little burro.

What does it mean to be astounding? It means having the audacity to surprise people by going above and beyond their expectations. To surpass their preconceived ideas about you and their assumptions of what you can bring to the world. You dazzle others with your unique abilities to defy the odds, giving them something to talk about. And you create a memorable legacy. This is a mark of true creative leadership—whether you are a CEO, an entrepreneur, a stay-at-home parent . . . or a burro. Finding a way to distinguish yourself creates a path of long-run success.

Brighty was just one donkey among hundreds of wild burros in the Grand Canyon. Truth be told, at the same time Brighty was making a name for himself, there were also countless domesticated donkeys who worked in the mines and carried gear for tourists. But this pancake-eating donkey surprised everyone by living both free *and* tame, without any limits, and beyond what was expected.

He became an unlikely hero.

He stood out.

He touched people's hearts.

Improbable, remarkable, unforgettable. These are characteristics of the Donkey Principle in action. As you lean in to your calling—to deliver the meaningful work that only you can do—the world will be astounded by your contribution.

IMPROBABLE

Have the audacity to surprise those who underestimate you.

Exceed expectations.

Be an underdog.

Be the one who defeats the odds, the one who shatters assumptions.

Be the improbable success story.

There is great power in being underestimated. When you're not expected to achieve something of note, you've actually been given a secret gift. Those who carry the burden of great expectations run the risk of disappointing themselves as well as those who have set those expectations in the first place. Their target is fixed, and achieving anything less is seen as failure. Anything *other* than that target is considered a miss.

You, on the other hand, have no such limitations. You have the opportunity to chart your own course and create your own targets. Being improbable gives you the gift of time—time to learn your craft, to scout the landscape, and to build your network of heroes, helpers, and herds. You can be resourceful and creative in finding solutions that exceed expectations—without external pressure to "succeed."

With nothing to lose, you can take a chance on a "moon shot," a near-impossible goal or ambition that has been written off by others—but offers you an opportunity to surprise the critics.

Alison Lumbatis, founder and CEO of Outfit Formulas, became a fashion blogger at age forty when she discovered her passion for helping women find their worthiness through wardrobes—an improbable path for someone who spent her career as an engineer. Alison was informed early on by a successful influencer that she would never make money with her blog because she didn't follow the traditional blogger business model of posting new clothing and outfits in order to earn affiliate commissions.

But that never felt authentic to Alison's own shopping habits, so she continued to post outfits that she "closet shopped" instead. Turns out, that influencer was right. She *didn't* make money from that, but as Alison told me, "What happened is something even better! I created a program for women that allowed them to work within their own budgets and create outfits from their closets. Instead of making money via the traditional model, I now have a business that creates over seven figures in revenue and employs a team of ten women to support it." Incredible!

Alison's improbable path allowed her to build a successful company that not only aligns with her values but serves and helps others as well.

I bet you've defied some odds of your own to get to where

you are now. Perhaps a well-meaning person has discouraged you from aiming too high. Maybe right now you're struggling to believe in your ability to achieve your own unlikely dream. Perhaps someone convinced you that you did not have the talent, aptitude, background, education, connections, or resources to create your path to success.

Prove them wrong.

Remember that donkeys *eat* improbability for breakfast. They are able to do the impossible—one intrepid step at a time—by taking alternate routes to their destination. When you feel discouraged, keep in mind that *many* great leaders and achievers were written off by others. From Winston Churchill, once considered a washed-up politician who went on to lead Great Britain in World War II, to Volodymyr Zelensky, a former comedic actor who became the president of Ukraine and stood against a Russian invasion, heroes find their way to the top in spite of low expectations placed on them.

A stray burro at the bottom of the Grand Canyon? Yep, one improbable story. He challenged expectations with his oversized personality and charm, winning hearts and minds along the way. Brighty reminds us that being underestimated can be a powerful place to start. When you decide that odds can favor the risk-takers, you begin to embrace the improbable and seek to surprise and dazzle the naysayers.

Dig Deeper

★ Why not? (This is where asking "Why not?" really shines.) Why *not* be the one who defies expectations and delivers a surprise finish? What expectations do you think people have of you now? What would surprise them most?

_____

_____

_____

_____

_____

_____

★ What would it take to move your dreams from "impossible" to "possible?"

_____

_____

_____

_____

_____

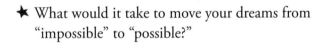

★ When will you take action? Set a start and finish date to complete the first of your goals. What goal tops your list? What other goals loom large in your mind?

_____

_____

_____

★ Starting date for my first goal: _____
   Finish date: _____

REMARKABLE

Stand out in a crowd.
     Leave people talking about you.
     Delight others by being extraordinary.
     Brighty was one of hundreds of wild donkeys living around the Grand Canyon, and yet he alone stood out. He was remarkable. After all, he was a *pancake-loving* burro. You see, it didn't take much to get people talking. Simply by doing something out of the ordinary, Brighty was a topic of conversation. No one had ever met a donkey that ate hotcakes, and his antics brought smiles to their faces. Visitors to the canyon were astounded that a wild donkey would freely give rides to children and help them with their chores. They

laughed when he bucked adults off his back or refused to budge for demanding teenagers. And that he could judge a person's character? Now, that was something to talk about!

I've met many remarkable people in my life. They are individuals who surprise others with their unusual interests or abilities. My friend Becki is an amazing ski instructor in Idaho. She's a mom of five and grandmother of two . . . and an amputee. Diagnosed with a rare cancer as a teenager, her left leg was amputated at the thigh before she graduated from high school. She's never let that stop her from pursuing the sports she loves, from running to cycling to skiing and everything in between. Remarkable.

I will never forget my husband's cardiac surgeon from almost thirty years ago who wore unusual and interesting ties with his lab coat. The ties reflected his wide range of interests—from fishing lures to comic book heroes—and they *never* failed to spark a comment as he made his morning rounds. In a recent conversation, my husband and I could *still* recall specific designs that caught our attention. He brought a smile to his patients and alleviated their anxieties simply by choosing remarkable ties each day.

I once had a dentist who looked exactly like Clint Eastwood. So much so, that he took advantage of the resemblance and used it as a key part of his marketing strategy. There were billboards around the city that played up the likeness as part of my dentist's personal brand. That definitely got people talking.

Then there was an older friend named Peggy who loved to

host parties. She planned them all year long, making her parties into memorable events that people recalled for years afterward. She taught classes in home entertaining that were always well attended by younger women (and men) who found her exuberance for parties contagious.

We often underestimate how little it takes to be remarkable. Many times, it is as simple as going the extra mile to show kindness or do something noteworthy. President George H. W. Bush was well known for his personal, handwritten letters. Every day, he jotted thank-you notes to people, from office assistants to world leaders, to express appreciation for both small and seemingly insignificant things to big important things on the global stage. He saw it as a simple way to connect with others, yet we are still talking about it today.

Now is a good time to ask yourself, "What sets me apart? What am I known for, and how can I delight others?"

Being remarkable is not about being the best at what you do in your professional field or exploiting a branding scheme. It's about pursuing interests, skills, and experiences that enhance your life and enlarge your sphere of influence and culture. When you step out of your comfort zone by saying yes to a new creative outlet, committing to a new habit, or finally embracing your idiosyncrasies, you begin to move from ordinary to extraordinary. Taking a further step to go public with your pursuits and interests can put you into a league of your own.

Being remarkable means that conversations are started. Connections are made. Perceptions are changed.

Give people something to talk about.

Dig Deeper

★ Why not say yes to an activity or hobby that you're interested in but have put off? What might that be?

_____

_____

_____

★ What would "being remarkable" look like for you? What would you like people to say about you when you leave the room?

_____

_____

_____

★ When will you make a date to do something out of the ordinary? What will you choose to do?

_____

_____

_____

UNFORGETTABLE

Be a person of impact by connecting with people's emotions.

Dare to be unforgettable.

What is it that makes a person memorable? Is it just being unusual or novel? Is it found in creating an exciting experience? Is it in saying something profound?

Or is being unforgettable found in something deeper?

Maya Angelou is credited with saying, "I've learned that people will forget what you said, people will forget what you did, but *people will never forget how you made them feel.*"

Little Brighty is remembered long after being gone because he touched people's hearts. There was something about him that provoked an emotional response in everyone he came in contact with. He was free to run wild, and yet he stayed with people and delighted them with his antics. Living as he did on his own terms reminded people of their own ability to live free from the shackles of expectation and imagine a kind of life that is filled with discovery and joy. People fell in love with both his untamed spirit and his vulnerability, finding something special in Brighty that endeared him to them.

Brighty made people happy.

Being unforgettable means connecting with people's emotions, and this can only happen when you are your authentic donkey-self. It involves a bit of personal risk by being vulnerable, but the reward is a deep, lasting connection with others. It's why, if you ask someone to name an unforgettable person, they are not likely to name a celebrity but rather someone who has personally impacted them. Often it is a parent or relative who has seen them for who they are—and who accepts and loves them anyway—making a lasting emotional impact on them. It may be a teacher who connected on a more profound level than just a classroom setting, someone who inspired them or helped them to see their own value.

Being an unforgettable person is one who

- is sincere
- shows emotion
- shares their stories
- listens and *sees* other people
- affirms others
- is not pretentious
- is genuine
- pays attention
- knows what matters
- shows empathy
- makes others feel valued

Fred Rogers of *Mr. Rogers' Neighborhood* was just such an unforgettable person. His television show, which aired on public television from 1968 until 2001, reflected his deep love for children and their emotional well-being. Unlike other children's shows which focused on learning and school-readiness, Mr. Rogers focused on the emotional and physical health of children through his calm demeanor, kind voice, and willingness to talk about difficult subjects like death, divorce, race, disability, and loss.

An ordained Presbyterian minister, Fred Rogers felt that the space between him and a child watching his show on TV was a "sacred space," so he approached each show with care and thoughtfulness. As a result, he helped millions of children and their families grow in empathy, kindness, and understanding. He helped them deal with topics that were important to them, validating their feelings and modeling acceptance. Mr. Rogers found a way to emotionally connect, through the medium of television, with sincerity and vulnerability. Somehow, his young viewers could sense that he saw them and understood their world. He will never be forgotten.

Improbable, remarkable, unforgettable. Being astounding is within your reach. You don't have to set a world record for speed or become a viral sensation on the internet for your dance moves. What it takes is mining your personal story for your own unlikely trajectory—notice the ways you've surprised yourself and others, embrace your distinctiveness, and determine to make deep connections with others.

Dig Deeper

★ Why not let down your guard and have an honest conversation with someone you care about? Who would that person be?

_____

_____

_____

★ What would it take for you to be unforgettable? What would it look like to be unforgettable in your personal world? Your professional world?

_____

_____

_____

_____

_____

_____

_____

_____

_____

_____

★ When will you pursue this? It seems there is never a good time for reaching out to let someone know you care. If you've put off writing that letter or making that phone call, do it this week. Jot down some ideas of what you'd like to say here.

DELIVER
YOUR WORK

CHAPTER 9

ASCEND

"On your marks, get set, GO!"

The athletes spring into action at the sound of the starter's gun, running a twenty-one-mile race over rugged mountain terrain. The participants all compete together—male and female, young and old, large and small—in teams of two: one human and one donkey. Like their teammates, the donkeys (called burros in the American West) range in size from mammoth, to standard, to miniature. This is a pack burro race, the official summer heritage sport of Colorado, and *yes*, it's a thing! Rules are simple: Each donkey must carry a weighted pack that includes a mining pan, a pickax, and shovel—just as the donkeys of historic mining days did. Everyone runs with their donkey (no riding allowed), and each person must hold a lead rope the whole way. If the rope is dropped, the competitor must go back to where they dropped it and begin again. It's both a celebration of the history of mining towns and a showcase for the athleticism of the amazing animals who were part of the gold rushes.

Folklore has it that the first race began when two prospectors raced down the mountain into town to stake their claims on a vein of gold . . . their donkeys alongside them. The first *official* race started in 1949 in Fairplay, Colorado, and since then, people from all around the world arrive in Western mining towns to participate in this extreme sport. While there are prizes handed out for the teams with the fastest time, every team that crosses the finish line achieves the satisfaction of completing a hard-won goal.

Shane Weigand, a founding member of the New Mexico Pack Burro team and a board member of the Western Pack Burro Ass-ociation, has traveled to the neighboring state with a six-year-old donkey named Comet. As a bowhunter, Shane initially got interested in burros as a means to pack elk meat out of the mountains, but once he got a couple of his own donkeys, he became an enthusiast for the whole pack burro tradition.

"Burros are so much a part of the history of the West," he tells me as we talk about his experiences. "Nearly every photo of the old mountain mining towns has donkeys in them; they were everywhere."

Shane's bowhunting expeditions provide an abundance of quality time with his burros—hiking miles into the backcountry, sleeping under the stars together, and working as a team. He says donkeys have a unique presence about them that make them uniquely suited for the treks. Calm, with a natural instinct for the trail, the burros seem to understand their own strength and ability to handle the work and the challenges of the mountains. They appear to be completely in the moment, able to enjoy the adventure and, of course, sometimes take advantage of the alpine grasses and shrubs for snacks along the way. There is a quiet confidence that does not require them to jockey for position or attention. "They are simply amazing animals who aren't recognized for their contributions enough," Shane says.

With a laugh, he continues, "One of the challenges of working with burros, whether in the backcountry or when racing, is simply the way they navigate situations along the way." Often when a donkey approaches something he is unsure of, he will simply stop—much to the frustration of the handler. Balking like this is often confused with being ornery, something that is easy to mock or make fun of. However, a burro has learned that there is great benefit in pausing. It's a classic move that puts the power dynamic under their control. "You definitely have to check your ego when you're competing," says Shane.

The burro races take place in small towns throughout Colorado and the Southwest, and Shane knew he wanted to be part of the experience. He raced with a few other burros before adopting Comet from the Bureau of Land Management (an agency overseen by the US Department of the Interior), and now the two of them are building their athletic partnership as they go.

Shane knows that learning to pace himself and Comet is the key to persevering in a long-haul race. "Once you get past the first hour, which is full of adrenaline and excitement, you try to settle into a pace that's sustainable. You have to remember that your burro doesn't care about a prize. He is in it because *you're* in it, and you have to work together to get across the finish line. The donkeys enjoy the satisfaction of completing the job with you."

Donkeys, whether racing up mountain paths, trekking into the backcountry, or packing gold out of a mine, know their own pace; they are sure-footed and swift but can't be forced to hurry against their will. They are aware of their own presence and confident in their own ability to manage the terrain. Finally, they know that pausing gives them the opportunity to think through their next steps.

How will *you* ascend the mountain that is your calling? By remembering your pace, your presence, and the power of the pause.

PACE

Don't be in a hurry. Settle into a sustainable speed for the long haul.

Find the pace that works for *you*.

While donkeys demonstrate their athleticism in pack burro races, their greatest strength lies not in speed, but in the actual *pacing*. Each donkey athlete will gallop, trot, and walk (yep, they might even balk) along the path, and that's part of the charm and challenge of events like this. They work with their human partners to achieve a sustainable pace for the changing terrain—from paved roads to rocky trails, mountain passes, and steep ravines. Often, the burro leads the human and sets the speed, making the decisions about how to approach the trail. This requires a level of trust that is built through consistent training and time.

"It's always a good idea to find another team you can keep pace with," Shane Weigand tells me as we continue the conversation. "On the trail you can create a 'pod' with others. Letting one burro get out in front of the group helps the others stay engaged and moving forward." That's not a bad strategy for real-life pacing as well. Finding others who are going the same direction can help keep you motivated to stay the course when you feel like quitting.

Can donkeys run fast? Of course, they can. But donkeys aren't necessarily built for speed.

They are built for endurance.

They are built to *deliver the goods*.

And this requires pacing.

It means slowing down to conserve energy and finding a rhythm that works, one that will last. Any distance runner will tell you that setting a manageable pace is the key to staying the course. Starting off at full speed is guaranteed to use up the fuel you'll need for the later legs of the journey.

Unfortunately, most of us feel like we are being asked to live at breakneck speed. Technology has made our lives easier, but it has also created a 24/7 environment in which we are on call at all hours of the day. Work doesn't stop at 5:00 p.m.—it invades our evenings and weekends, interrupts our sleep at night, and awakens us earlier than our alarms. We feel that we must jump on every opportunity and be available to the demands of an ever-increasing load of responsibilities. As a result, our productivity actually suffers, and our ability to deliver meaningful work into the world is reduced.

Learning the value of pacing yourself usually happens after you reach the burnout stage—the point at which you can't take another step. That's when it's past time to reevaluate priorities and set boundaries so that you can live a productive and meaningful life, not one that's overloaded and forced. A better approach is to *start off* with the kind of mindset that looks at the long haul and determines how best to finish well.

In her book *The Long Game: How to Be a Long-Term Thinker in a Short-Term World*, Dorie Clark says this: "Understand what it really takes to accomplish your goals. Too many people get discouraged that they're not progressing faster, simply because they never took the time to ask questions or discover how long it's taken others to succeed. Develop a clear picture first so you can pace yourself and set realistic goals."

Once you realize that life is not about winning the race but about delivering your good work to the world, you can begin to think about what pace is sustainable for you. You can begin to create a life that is built to serve you and the world around you in beautiful ways—on your own time and on your own terms.

Dig Deeper

★ Why not evaluate the pace of your life? Does your current project/life feel like a race that's out of control? Is winning your goal? Or is "packing"—bringing your best work to the world—the goal?

_____

_____

_____

_____

★ What would it look like to set your own pace? What rhythm feels best for you?

_____

_____

_____

_____

_____

_____

_____

★ How does setting a pace impact what you do today toward that goal? What can you eliminate?

_____

_____

_____

_____

_____

_____

_____

PRESENCE

Trust your instincts. Believe in the power of your own presence.

Most of us move through the world comparing ourselves to others and feeling inadequate. We *feel* like donkeys in a world that celebrates racehorses—those glossy winners who effortlessly glide to personal and professional victory. We give credence to the voices that tell us we don't measure up and that we can't compete. In doing so we diminish our own presence in the world. It's a recipe for inertia, a surefire way to implode before we even begin.

Perhaps you, too, have been conditioned to accept a narrative of success that is far too narrow. "Be shiny. Be slick. Be the fastest horse." You've been trying to compete on a track that you weren't created for—one that circles endlessly until an elite few are crowned winners.

But this isn't what you are made for at all!

Instead, you are created to be a caretaker of the gold in the wild lands of freedom. You get to choose your course. You get to take it off-road. You are equipped to be nimble along treacherous pathways and fearless on mountain tops. This is not for the shiny and slick, but for the dusty and sure-footed.

There is power in this kind of presence.

You bring this kind of presence to the world.

You own the real estate you take up.

Your existence is powerful, and it's not measured by someone else's standard.

Once you discover the depth of your own presence, you can begin to trust your instincts as you make your own path forward—no groomed track necessary. You can stand tall in your donkey-self.

I'm reminded of Chase Jarvis, who attended college on a soccer scholarship and dove into academics with the plan of securing a spot at a prestigious medical school. One week before his college graduation, however, his grandfather suddenly passed away from a heart attack, leaving behind a small collection of cameras and lenses for Chase. It wasn't much of an inheritance at face value, but it was enough to refocus Chase's grief toward a creative pursuit that would dramatically alter his life's path.

With determination and hard work, he became world-renowned for his photography, and he went on to design CreativeLive.com, a platform dedicated to helping others follow their creative dreams. Chase bucked the "prescribed" track for success and created his own path through unknown terrain because he trusted his instincts. He writes, "The whisper of intuition telling us what we're meant to do and how we're meant to live comes from within, but it leads away into the unknown. Once I finally started listening to the call, I found myself on a new path. Not the path designed by my career counselor, encouraged by my parents, or suggested by society. My own."

This is what standing tall in your presence can look like.

Amy Cuddy, author of *Presence: Bringing Your Boldest Self to Your Biggest Challenges*, tells us, "Presence is the state of being attuned to, and able to comfortably express, our true thoughts, feelings, values, and potential. . . . Presence emerges when we feel personally powerful, which allows us to be acutely attuned to our most sincere selves."

What are your instincts telling you to do? Run? Lie down? Fight? Or . . . show up? Listen? Work? Dig deep? Quiet the external voices so you can pay attention to your own internal compass. This takes courage and practice. Let go of who you're *not* and opt out of the races you're *not* supposed to run. This lets you embrace your true strengths and capabilities and frees you to do things that are congruent with your values. If you follow through, you will stand tall in your own presence.

Dig Deeper

★ Why not get off the groomed track that someone else has made for you and choose your own path? Ideally, where would you like that path to take you?

_____

_____

_____

★ What would it look like to trust your own instincts? What would it take for you to be able to pay attention to your gut feeling about things?

_____

_____

_____

_____

_____

_____

_____

★ When will you decide to act on what you instinctively know to be true? Why is *now* a good time?

_____

_____

_____

_____

_____

_____

_____

PAUSE

Learn the power of pausing.

It's no secret: Donkeys often balk. They stop right in their tracks and refuse to move.

They simply will. not. go.

This can cause frustration and embarrassment to the person trying to get them to do what they're told. I can't tell you how many times I've tried to pull my donkey Flash forward when he has inexplicably decided to stop walking with me. The worst is when it happens in front of people I might be hoping to impress. Or as Shane Wiegand tells it with a rueful grin, "When you're trying to cross a finish line."

Why *do* donkeys balk? Are they downright stubborn? Or is it because they are stupid?

It's actually neither of these things. Pausing is an instinctive move that puts the power of choice back in their corner.

You see, donkeys often stop because they may be uncertain of what is ahead. They may not trust the instructions or the instructor. They may be tired. There may be something causing them pain or discomfort. Or . . . they may have a better idea.

Pausing is a donkey's way of clarifying his choices. Rather than rushing ahead, he is taking a moment to consider which action to take. He is communicating that he will not be forced into a decision or an action without thinking it through.

We can all stand to learn the power of the pause.

How many rushed decisions have you made, only to regret them later? How often have you felt pressured into doing something you didn't want to do, purchased something you didn't need, or made promises you couldn't keep?

I once purchased a very expensive vacuum cleaner from two salespeople who had been recommended by a friend. The sales duo spent hours at my house, showing me all the bells and whistles of this machine, which weighed as much as a rhino and was just about as unwieldy. And then they stayed another hour, pressing me to sign the contract. (All the while, my toddlers were crying for attention.) Rushed, pressured, and knowing my friend had bought one, I agreed to monthly payments that stretched our young family's budget. If only I had paused, I would have reconsidered. I would have given myself space to think clearly and say no. I wouldn't have mentally cussed every time I wrangled that vacuum for the next ten years, just to get my money's worth.

A donkey pauses, much to the chagrin of others. A wise companion will wait until the donkey decides it is safe, smart, or beneficial to move forward.

Pausing takes courage. When you listen to your gut, it will often warn you of danger ahead, or alert you to an untrustworthy person, or signal that a business deal seems off somehow. It gives you margin to reflect, to proceed with gratitude, or to weigh your values. Pausing makes you keenly aware of your own presence to give you the gift of space and time—so that you can make the best decision before taking the next step. Fair warning: Sometimes this response will frustrate those around you who want you to hurry up and agree with them, and you may be called "stubborn" in the process. Alas, this is the burden we donkeys bear.

But remember, you're not stubborn; you're *resolved* to live with integrity and honor. And sometimes it takes a midcourse pause to find those values that create a foundation of good decision-making.

Pause.

Almost every decision you'll ever make will still be there after you've had a moment, or a day, or a week to think about it.

Dig Deeper

★ Why not pause:
   - on a relationship that feels off?
   - your busy schedule to make time and regroup?
   - at being forced into a decision that goes against your better judgment?
   - before tweeting or sending the next email or text?

★ Write down how pausing could make a positive impact on your current situation.

_____

_____

_____

_____

_____

★ What would it be like to give yourself time and space to think clearly? What would it hurt to tell someone, "Let me sleep on this decision"? Record how this might feel.

_____

_____

_____

_____

_____

★ When will you carve out specific time to reflect before moving forward? What needs to be adjusted in your routine to make that a reality?
Date: _____

You are created
to be a caretaker
of the gold
in the wild lands
of freedom.

CHAPTER 10

ASSIST

Alfa and Beto make their way up the treacherous mountainside in single file, with Alfa in the lead. Beto shakes his long ears and keeps his eyes on Alfa's back feet as he picks his way forward through the dense brush that nearly obscures the muddy path going up, up, up into the jungle.

"You can do it!"

A man named Luis Soriano leads Alfa, shouting encouragement to the two burros who have been carrying their precious cargo for hours. They are almost to their destination: a remote village in the mountains of Colombia. Alfa and Beto are the transporters for the "biblioburro" (loosely translated in Spanish as "the donkey library"), assisting Luis by bringing a load of books to the children who live in this small settlement.

Luis, a teacher who grew up in the small town of La Gloria, is passionate about bringing books to children.

"The children are (always) very excited because when we come it is a day of colours, princes, princesses and emotion," he said as reported by a British newspaper. "What we try to do is construct a laboratory of imagination."

As a kid, Luis discovered a whole world beyond his village through reading books, and as a result he pursued an education in Spanish literature. As an elementary school teacher, he knows how important it is for children to have access to books. He sees education as the only path forward for a generation of kids who are otherwise at the mercy of local militia forces and drug cartels that prey on the uneducated villagers. In response to these threats, he began assembling a small library of his own books to share. He modified saddle packs that were meant for carrying water into packs that could hold the books "library style" with spines facing out, enlisted his donkeys' help, and took off for a village several hours away. Greeted like a celebrity, Luis now has thousands of books which are housed in the area's first-ever library in La Gloria, opened in 2000. He personally chooses the titles he thinks the children will enjoy the most and always brings a selection of read-aloud stories that he can share. The children lean in and hang on his every word, and he encourages them to learn to read the books he leaves for them.

During the climb Luis can see that Beto's pack has become loose and unbalanced. The weight of the books has pulled the pack backward, and now that the ground has leveled out, he is struggling to regain his footing. Luis jostles the pack into place and cinches up the strap. He rearranges the books so they are more evenly distributed, and checks Beto's body to see if the harness has chafed his skin. Next, he moves on to Alfa and sees that she simply needs her pack shifted forward and she is good to go.

Over the past twenty-five years, Luis has refined the packs so that he can ride atop them as they travel into dense jungles, across steep ravines, and along some of the most difficult trails imaginable. The two donkeys have been his partners the whole time, doing what they do best—shouldering and sharing the load.

Donkeys are *made* for service. Assisting is their game, their jam, their joy. Their compact size allows them to be nimble over rough terrain and steady along dangerous routes. Able to accommodate heavy loads, they settle into a pace that is sustainable for the long haul.

We sometimes forget that we, too, are made for service. We often get so focused on being "the fastest one out of the gate" or we get so wrapped up in work that keeps us busy that we don't actually do the things that bring the most good to the world—or what ultimately brings us the most fulfillment. It turns out that we are *built* for serving others, and we work best when we are able to share the teamwork so that no one person is overloaded. Sometimes those loads must be shifted, harnesses adjusted, and tasks evaluated in order to be most productive and effective.

Shouldering, sharing, shifting. Stepping into our roles as service animals brings out the best in us and helps the world flourish in our wake.

SHOULDER THE LOAD

Be a service animal.

Don't be afraid to shoulder a load for someone else.

You are *made* for service. Designed with sturdy legs and a low center of gravity, donkeys' unique physical structure allows them to carry heavy loads and makes them perfect for shouldering packs or pulling wagons or plows. Domesticated around 3000 BC, donkeys have been responsible for advancing humankind's commerce and trade, making such routes as the famed Silk Road possible with their ability to travel long distances in difficult conditions.

Currently there are an estimated 42 million working donkeys worldwide supporting the livelihoods of over 250 million people. Playing a critical role in agriculture, transportation, and commercial and industrial work, the donkey is the poster child of what it means to serve in ways only donkeys can.

When you think about being a "service animal," it's important to remember that only you can shoulder the work that *you* were designed to do—in the way only you can do it. When you take your ideas, your passion, and your skill sets and you focus on a need that *you* can meet, that's when the magic happens.

That's what Dr. Sanduk Ruit did. He was born into a poor family in a remote village in Nepal with no school. His father was educated and arranged for Sanduk to learn basic Nepalese, English, and math. Sanduk did well with his lessons, and when he was seven, his father enrolled him in a Jesuit boarding school in Darjeeling, nearly a hundred miles away. After finishing his early education, Sanduk went on to secondary school and further studies in India before completing his specialty in ophthalmology at two medical colleges. As a highly trained eye surgeon, he could have pursued a lucrative career in the United States or elsewhere, but he felt that all people deserve to have the gift of vision, whether they can pay for it or not. So he began to work among the poorest people in Nepal, perfecting a sutureless surgical technique that removes cataracts and replaces them with lenses he produces in his own labs. To date, he has performed more than 180,000 surgeries, giving sight—and productive lives—back to people whose disability prevented them from working and contributing to the well-being of their families and communities. Dr. Ruit is deeply committed to serving the poorest communities and giving their residents a second chance at life.

As amazing as Dr. Ruit's example is, shouldering a load in service to others doesn't have to be part of a full-time job, or attached to a corporate or business venture, or turned into a nonprofit organization. It can be done on your own time and in your own way—using the gifts, resources, and abilities that you have. Find a specific need you are suited for and take it on.

I think of my daughter Meghan, an early childhood music specialist, who makes music education for preschoolers available online at an affordable price. Her small Flourish Music company, operating out of her living room, is the result of her love of teaching, and her unique skill sets make it possible to reach out to kids and parents with something she is passionate about.

Then there is Kwesia, also known as @citygirlinnature on social media. As a young woman of color who grew up in an inner-city area of South East London, she has taken her enthusiasm for nature and embarked on introducing other city kids to the outdoors through Twitter, YouTube, and in-person expeditions. She carries nature to those who need it, with her unique style and ability.

The ways to serve others are endless. So square your shoulders. Ask yourself what kind of service *you* are made for. Your unique skills and interests equip you to carry goods, services, and assistance to your herd and the world beyond.

Dig Deeper

★ Why not explore ways to use your unique skill set to serve others? What forms of service are a natural fit for you?

_____

_____

_____

_____

_____

★ What would it look like to serve your clients and customers well? How about someone who cannot pay or does not have access to your services?

_____

_____

_____

_____

_____

★ When will you begin to serve? Have a brainstorming session with yourself to investigate ways to serve. What date will you put on your calendar for this exercise? When you start exploring, write down the possibilities you discover.

_____

_____

_____

_____

_____

_____

_____

_____

_____

_____

_____

_____

_____

_____

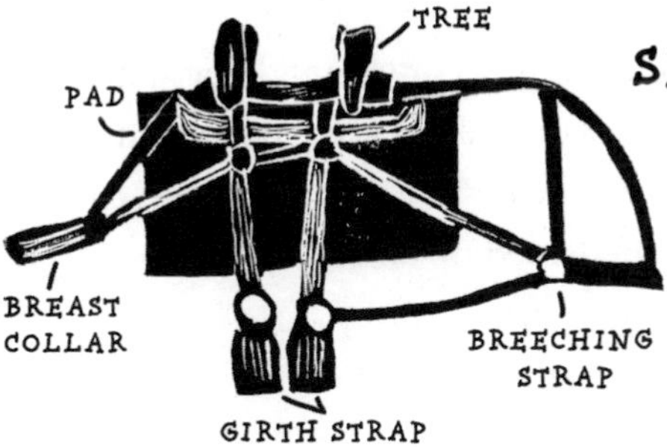

Labels on diagram:
- TREE
- PAD
- BREAST COLLAR
- BREECHING STRAP
- GIRTH STRAP

SHIFT THE LOAD

Effective work requires good systems.

Ill-fitting harnesses and unbalanced loads can hamper your ability to serve.

You can serve longer, carry more weight, and travel farther when you are properly equipped to handle the load.

Sometimes when a job becomes too difficult, the problem is not that the workload is too heavy—it's that the systems need adjusting to be able to handle it. Once things are shifted around and the right processes are found, often the work gets done more efficiently.

Donkeys have impressive stamina and strength, but they are often given ill-fitting harnesses that are not designed for the job. Then they are expected to pull or carry more than the maximum weight while being chafed or rubbed raw by the straps or traces. Sometimes the harness may be designed for a completely different animal, or cobbled together by its owner, and the unbalanced weight of the wagon puts unnecessary pressure on the animal's back or shoulders, creating painful sores.

And here's where a donkey's greatest assets, resilience and resolve, can work against him. You see, donkeys (like some people

I know) are extremely stoic. They rarely complain. They don't show the stress they are under. They don't express pain or exhaustion. They just continue to work and serve . . . while more burdens keep piling up, until they are lamed by illness or overwork.

Does this sound like you, my friend?

Shifting the load means recognizing where your pain points are and finding ways to relieve them. When you take on the responsibility of serving others, there is often an initial joy that carries you through the first season of work. However, as time goes on, you may become burned out, burdened by the needs you're trying to meet, and living in an unbalanced way that isn't sustainable. You may be rubbed raw by an ill-fitting system or workflow that was never designed for you.

Donkeys often need others to step in and help. Brooke is a nonprofit organization that assists donkeys, other working equines, and their owners around the world. One of their major initiatives is to teach proper harnessing and provide affordable tack so that the animals can work effectively without pain. This initiative has many positive outcomes: Not only does the donkey have a better work structure, but there is an economic boost for the owner as well. A pain-free, healthy donkey with properly fitting harnesses and appropriate loads is able to better sustain the livelihoods of the people who depend on them.

During the COVID-19 pandemic, businesses and organizations had to adjust the way they served their customers and navigated the changes happening. Many experienced the pain of no in-person shopping, servicing, or working, so they shifted to online strategies that allowed them to continue to keep their doors open even when people could not physically be present. They focused on creating a balanced load by changing their systems, shifting their loads, and looking for ways to change how they "pulled their wagon." The result for many was innovation—outside-the-box thinking and new strategies that could propel them forward.

What can be shifted in your work life so that there isn't too much weight in one area? What is rubbing you raw instead of giving you strength? Being clear about how your work serves people in specific ways helps give you motivation to make adjustments that create a sustainable effort.

Dig Deeper

★ If serving others through your work seems too hard or heavy, why not take a look at your pain points and see if adjustments can be made? Start by identifying them here.

_____

_____

_____

_____

★ What would shifting your processes around look like? What would the workload feel like without pain?

_____

_____

_____

_____

_____

_____

_____

_____

_____

_____

_____

_____

★ When might you be able to assess your systems for serving and make appropriate changes for sustainable efforts? Set a date here:

_____

SHARE THE LOAD

You need partners to help share the work.

Give yourself permission to ask for help.

Give yourself permission to *accept* help.

Alfa and Beto, the two Colombian biblioburros, are partners in the effort to serve children in remote villages. They are able to carry twice as many books to eager kids as one donkey could do alone. Working together, they keep each other company when the trails are difficult, and they spur each other on to complete their mission. As social creatures who excel in their task of assisting Luis Soriano, they benefit the village children by their willingness to share the load, doubling the potential for education and growth.

It's tempting to think that we are nimble, flexible, and capable enough on our own for the task we are called to or dream about. After all, bringing others in to help may mean we give up control and have to spend time teaching someone else the ropes. But sharing the load, no matter what the endeavor, is vital to the sustainability of the effort over the long haul. Going it alone will only get you so far. When you bring others in to help carry the burdens or pull the wagon or accomplish a goal, the weight of the effort is distributed so that no one person is overwhelmed.

The stoic donkey in you is sometimes not even aware that you are suffering under the heavy weights you carry. You are accustomed to being uncomfortable, having too much to do, and not having enough time to rest and recharge. It might even be a badge of honor. But let's face it, donkeys are easily taken advantage of and all too often are abused, simply because they keep going without complaining.

But serving others—through caregiving, your occupation, your business, your philanthropy, or ministry—isn't meant to kill you in the process. Giving of yourself should bring satisfaction and joy. After all, this is what you are made for!

You will almost always benefit from having others come alongside you or from coming alongside someone else to help bear *their* burden. Sharing the load may look like rethinking work responsibilities, assigning tasks, delegating, or simply learning to communicate better. It could look like finding a doctor or clinician who can partner with you to tackle mental health or physical challenges you may be facing. It might look like babysitting a friend's kids so *she* can get uninterrupted time to work or rest. It could mean hiring technical help in order to launch a new website. The point is that no one should go it alone. Fresh legs, strong shoulders, and teamwork make any task feel less burdensome and more fulfilling.

Your efforts can yield exponential results for those you serve when you share the load. Gold miners in the old American

West harnessed "burro trains" to bring load after load from deep in the mountains—multiplying the yield for every single trip. Working together means more treasure can be produced for the good of the world. Sometimes this is called "scaling up," a business concept that uses collaboration, sharing, networking, automating, and systematizing in order to grow and meet the needs of customers or clients. Whether you represent a business or an individual wanting to make an impact, scaling up simply means finding other donkeys, getting the right "harnesses" or systems, and each of you pulling together to create that change.

You are made for service: Assisting others is your game, your jam, and your joy.

Dig Deeper

★ Why not think of sharing as "scaling up" when it comes to your work? Why not step in and share someone else's load as *they* scale up? Who could you do that for?

_____

_____

_____

_____

_____

_____

★ What would it take to ask for help? What would it take for the work to be shared for maximum impact?

_____

_____

_____

_____

_____

_____

_____

★ When will you stop thinking like a solo operator and see your work as a communal effort for the greater good? What would satisfy you most when all is said and done?

_____

_____

_____

_____

_____

_____

_____

Stepping into our roles
as service animals
brings out the best in us
and helps the world
flourish in our wake.

CHAPTER 11

ASLEEP
& ASWIRL

A thunder of hooves breaks the stillness of the Texas morning, interrupting my thoughts. I am sitting beneath cedar trees just outside the pasture fence, a cup of coffee steaming on the small bistro table near my laptop and notes. I ponder the final chapter of this book, trying to decide which literary or otherwise famous donkey to highlight as the pièce de résistance. My mind clicks through the contenders: Platero, the central character in Juan Ramón Jiménez's Nobel prize–winning book *Platero and I*; Eeyore of Winnie-the-Pooh fame; Queen Elizabeth's favorite carriage donkey Jacquot; or Benjamin from George Orwell's *Animal Farm*. Or maybe Bottom from Shakespeare's *A Midsummer Night's Dream*? So many to choose from.

Following the sound of hoofbeats, I turn my attention to the far end of the pasture where my donkeys are in the thick of playing with each other. Dark brown miniature Henry is chasing his larger companion Flash by nipping at his heels. They race across the dusty ground, zigzagging along, and I can almost hear Flash saying, "Serpentine, serpentine," to himself as he tries to escape the teasing of his nimble friend.

Ears back, Flash finally skids to a stop and swirls around to face Henry, who pulls up short, eyes wide, and tries to back-pedal. Flash manages to bite Henry's mane before Henry shakes him off, turns, and kicks his back feet into Flash's solid chest. Now it's Flash's turn to give chase, and Henry is off as fast as his little legs can carry his portly body. He heads to the barn and grabs a black rubber feed dish with his mouth and lifts it high, just in time for Flash to crunch down on the other side of it for a game of tug-of-war. Dust rises up from the ground around them, giving their game a storybook glow in the morning light. Flash tires first, and he relinquishes the dish to Henry with a nod as if to say, "You win, buddy." Henry trots out into the field with the dish up over his face while the bigger donkey seems to chuckle with a quiet whinny at his silly playmate.

My coffee has cooled enough to sip as I watch the two burros who greet every morning with a romp like this one. Play is something they take seriously, a chance to "get their wiggles out," as I used to say about my children when they struggled to sit still or focus. A quick game of follow-the-leader in the yard or a chase around the house would often be just the thing my kids needed to self-regulate their attitudes and ability to listen. Laughter would ring out as a tickle fight might ensue, all of us collapsing on the floor in a heap of giggles. I watch the donkeys; both are considered adults—easily fourteen or fifteen years old now—and yet they play just as hard as youngsters do. I shake my head in amusement and return to my notes.

By midday, with the sun overhead and their bellies full from a morning of grazing, the two equines back themselves into their favorite spots beneath the trees and assume their napping positions: ears pointed backward atop their drooping heads, one back foot resting, bottom lips hanging low. It is the classic pose you might find on a Mexican burro figurine. Eyes closed, tail lazily swishing a fly, Flash loves his favorite shade tree near the barn, while Henry favors a variety of trees, based on his mood.

Filled with plenty of play and rest, the donkeys' days have a joyous rhythm to them. They are never bored, and they always seem to be in tune with their surroundings. This foundation makes them receptive to new skills and able to focus on whatever the day brings. These two live a life of relative leisure, with nothing but their inner circadian rhythms to tell them how to behave or how to regulate their activities. What donkeys do naturally is on full display.

Work, rest, play, joy.

What is good for donkeys is good for every creature, including humans. When we become overly focused on work and productivity, there may be short-term benefits—immediate gains and quick wins that feel good in the moment. But having long-haul impact requires rethinking that strategy in order to sustain a life that is wholehearted and healthy. There must be a balance of energy between what is expended and what is regularly replenished. We cannot run on empty indefinitely. Over the course of a lifetime, more can be accomplished through a sustainable lifestyle that includes taking care of your physical, mental, and emotional needs.

In order to build a life that sustains meaningful work and impacts others, you must look for ways to infuse it with enough rest and play that joy naturally arrives.

RESTFUL

You cannot live without proper rest.
Rest is nonnegotiable.
Rest is foundational to everything else.

"Things will look better in the morning," my mother used to say as she'd try to press the creases from my worried teenage brow. Knowing I was upset about a friendship gone awry or anxious about a test, she drew on an old saying (echoed by Mowgli in the movie *The Jungle Book*) as she gently tucked the covers around me. The age-old wisdom of "sleep on it" is supported by modern scientific research. During the course of a full night's sleep, the body and brain rest and repair themselves, resetting their ability to process emotion and enhancing your ability to solve problems. Moms, it seems, really do know best.

Matt Walker, author of *Why We Sleep: Unlocking the Power of Sleep and Dreams*, quotes entrepreneur E. Joseph Cossman, who says, "The best bridge between despair and hope is a good night's sleep."

In an age when every minute feels stretched to fit activities and obligations, rest can feel like a commodity that can be traded for increased productivity. *I can trade an hour of sleep for an hour of work or entertainment*, you think, but such a mentality sabotages your health, mental well-being, creativity, and even your longevity. Sleep deprivation is linked to issues like cardiovascular disease, cancer, high blood pressure, Alzheimer's disease, cognitive decline, and decreased life expectancy, just to name a few.

Rest allows us to accomplish more and gives us the ability to make better decisions about how we approach our lives, our work, and our service to others.

Flash and Henry's circadian rhythms tell them to simply

sleep when they feel sleepy. They instinctively know how much rest their bodies need, and they don't feel the least bit guilty about a midday doze. Their regular daytime naps under the shade trees supplement the sleep they get at night in the barn. We humans, like most creatures, benefit from napping as well. Research shows that a ten-to-twenty-minute nap is optimum for people to reduce sleepiness, improve learning and memory, and regulate emotions. Hourlong naps can have additional restorative benefits, including greater improvement in cognitive functioning. Some famous nappers include Aristotle, Leonardo da Vinci, Thomas Edison, Albert Einstein, Salvador Dali, Margaret Thatcher, Ronald Reagan, Morgan Freeman, and Bill Clinton . . . should you need further convincing.

Want to be a rebel? Want to resist the tides that pull you toward a life unmoored from personal balance? The most powerful way to take back your individual agency is to live a restful life. A restful life prioritizes generous sleep, regular daytime naps, and time spent in solitude, preferably in nature. By paying attention to your own circadian rhythm, you regain your sense of self and improve your well-being. Giving yourself the rest you need provides the foundation for long-haul strength and satisfaction.

Dig Deeper

★ If you struggle to have enough energy, focus, and cognitive strength, why not incorporate more rest into your life? What are your reasons for skipping rest?

_____

_____

_____

_____

_____

★ What would a restful life look like for you? Describe it in detail.

_____

_____

_____

_____

_____

★ What time will you go to sleep tonight? When will you wake up?

_____

_____

PLAYFUL

Play is the secret sauce to living a successful, long-haul life.

Play gives us access to curiosity and wonder.

It allows our minds to dwell in the land of imagination and possibilities.

For us donkeys, no day is complete without some play.

Meredith Hodges, world renowned donkey and mule trainer and founder of Lucky Three Ranch, says that "play is so important that it should even infuse their training and work. Development is not complete without a good balance of work and play." She emphasizes the integral role enjoyment has in learning and growing. Play makes for happy, healthy donkeys who can respond to new circumstances with openness and curiosity.

When I envision playfulness, I can't help but think of Donkey in the *Shrek* movies, who is always eager to inject fun into any situation. After he invites himself to stay with Shrek, the kindhearted and misunderstood ogre, Donkey can't wait to spend the night.

"We can stay up late, swapping manly stories, and in the morning, I'M MAKING WAFFLES!" He grins a big buck-toothed grin and gives his most appealing expression.

Donkey seems to understand the importance of being playful, even when the stakes are high. His playful attitude allows him to see the best in others and find ways to access his own potential.

Playfulness isn't just for donkeys and children; it's for all of us.

Incorporating more play into our lives means making time for things that bring delight and wonder, choosing activities that allow us to be curious and creative. For the productivity-driven person or organization, play can feel like a frivolous luxury, but research shows that opportunities for play create an atmosphere that encourages personal growth, problem solving, and overall satisfaction.

What kind of play, you ask? It doesn't matter, so long as the activities you choose provide you with a sense of fun and freedom. Whether that is riding a bike, running a marathon, knitting a sweater, tending indoor plants, going to museums, or listening to music—the list is endless. Play should spark your interest and engage your senses.

My son, Grayson, has taught me a lot about the value of play. He is an engineer who works hard in a meticulous science-driven industry, but he has learned the power of spending time away from the lab and outside in nature. He regularly hikes, climbs mountains, and camps just for fun, finding that it clears his mind and gives him energy to focus when he's back at work.

"We are built to play and built through play," says psychiatrist and author Dr. Stuart Brown, founder of the National

Institute for Play in Carmel Valley, California. He continues, "Remembering what play is all about and making it part of our daily lives are probably the most important factors in being a fulfilled human being. The ability to play is critical not only to being happy, but also to sustaining social relationships and being a creative, innovative person."

The Association for Psychological Science tells us, "Research has found evidence that play *at work* is linked with less fatigue, boredom, stress, and burnout in individual workers. Play is also positively associated with job satisfaction, sense of competence, and creativity."

Give yourself the gift of play. See it as a valued element of living your *goodest* life. Play reminds you that there is more to life than achieving your goals. It is about curiosity and creativity along the way. Play deepens your sense of identity, gives you a community of like-minded people, and fuels your capacity—when it *is* time to work—to work harder and smarter.

Like water, food, rest, and community, play is a nonnegotiable part of living the Donkey Principle. Play opens the gate to joy.

Dig Deeper

★ Why not add playtime to your life? If your first thought is *I don't have time!* list some of your reasons here. Then ask yourself whether or not they are true.

★ What would you do with a free afternoon? What would it take to free up a block of time, simply for something fun?

★ When will you schedule play this week? Is there someone you would enjoy doing it with?

JOYFUL

Embracing your inner donkey brings joy.

That's because when you embrace your inner donkey, you'll find—and flourish in—the meaningful work that you alone were created to do. It's the Donkey Principle.

True joy is found not in the acquisition of things but in the pursuit of a well-lived, long-haul life that includes serving others, expressing gratitude, and leaning in to your strengths. It values community, recognizes the past that brought you here, and asserts its vision for the future. Bob Goff puts it so succinctly in his book *Undistracted*: "Find your purpose, and you will experience more joy. The math is simple."

Joyful living isn't afraid of hard work or difficulties but realizes the only way to meet challenges head-on is with the kind of personal integrity and optimism that come when our outer person matches our inner self. It's when we realize that *who we are on the inside* is worthy of being lived on the outside.

Joy happens when we stop pretending to be something we are not, and instead become the truest version of who we *are*.

I'm reminded of Puzzle, the donkey in C. S. Lewis's *The Last Battle*. Puzzle has been convinced by others to pretend to be something he isn't by wearing a lion skin to fool them. He is deeply unhappy with this role but feels powerless to change it under the pressure to perform. When at last he finally has the courage to shed his fake persona, something magical happens.

> "Look!" said Jill suddenly. Someone was coming, rather timidly, to meet them; a graceful creature on four feet, all silvery-gray. And they stared at him for a whole ten seconds before five or six voices said all at once, "Why it's old Puzzle!" They had never seen him by daylight with the lion-skin off, and it made an extraordinary difference. He was himself now: a beautiful donkey with such a soft, gray coat and such a gentle, honest face that if you had seen him you would have done just what Jill and Lucy did—rushed forward and put your arms around his neck and kissed his nose and stroked his ears.

Puzzle, as himself, has become beautiful. His newfound softness and honesty elicit an immediate response of love and acceptance, a profound change that reflects his own transformation into his true identity. Only when he realizes he can be the donkey *that he already is* does he find that the world he'd always longed to be part of opens up to him.

Oh, the irony. Isn't it something?

When we choose to stop competing for attention, power, prestige, and success, and instead choose a lifestyle of meaningful connection and humble service, something amazing begins to unfold. We step off an exhausting, endless racetrack and into an adventure of our own making. We find the courage to forge a path through rocky terrain to find a gold mine of riches buried deep within us. Success, it turns out, isn't a trophy that's handed to the swiftest thoroughbreds, but it's an entire treasure trove of beauty that's delivered to the world by improbable, brave donkeys living their very goodest lives.

This is *you*.

You are made for this.

You are worthy of all the beauty life has to offer.

So kick up your heels! Buck a system you were never meant for.

Let your inner donkey run free—and into an unforgettable, remarkable, and wholly joyful adventure ahead.

Dig Deeper

★ If joy is not a hallmark of your life, why not? Why not go back through the pages of this book and mark up the areas that will bring more joy into your life and create a list here?

_____

_____

_____

_____

★ What would it take to finally embrace your inner donkey?

_____

_____

_____

_____

_____

_____

_____

_____

★ When will you get off the racetrack and forge your own path of adventure? Create a long-term calendar for the goals, ideas, and meaningful work you dream of! Make a commitment to begin plugging in dates, starting _____.

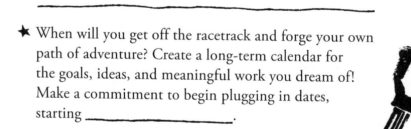

When you embrace
your inner donkey,
you will find and flourish
in the meaningful work
you were created to do.*

ASTERISK

Ah, there is always some fine print somewhere, isn't there? You know, the tiny text following an asterisk that states all the disclaimers such as

> *Individual results may vary.*
> *Not affiliated with any other Animal Principles, such*
> *as Zebras, Llamas, or Otters.*
> *Views expressed by any donkeys, whether real or*
> *fictional, may not reflect those of the author.*

In the case of this book, I offer my own disclaimer:*

* *Embracing your inner donkey may cause a sudden*
interest in eating grass, wiggling your ears, and rolling

in dirt. Not responsible for sudden urges to bray or snort while laughing. All references to "herds" are purely metaphorical and not representative of the people you choose to keep company with. Looking for excessive photos of donkeys in your social media feeds is considered normal and does not require medical or psychological intervention.

All kidding aside, I do want to say a few final words about finding and flourishing in the meaningful work you were created to do.

As I worked on the first drafts of this book, my editors encouraged me to organize the chapters into a framework that would make it easier for readers to follow. After trying a few different ideas, I came up with the acronym GOLD. It fit the theme of the book perfectly and allowed the chapters to flow in a cohesive manner.

G—Give Yourself Permission
O—Own Your Story
L—Lean In to Your Unique Strengths
D—Deliver Your Work

But something else happened that is worth sharing. Over the months of writing, I reviewed work I'd done in the past: I read long-forgotten journals tucked in drawers, workshop notes on my laptop, and PowerPoint presentations on thumb drives. Many of the notes came from my work within faith-based organizations, and some were from corporate events where I spoke. I looked at the coaching I'd done with clients and even thought back over the art I'd produced throughout the years.

A pattern emerged that caught me by surprise: the GOLD framework for personal growth and change was woven throughout *everything*.

But here is the kicker: I did not realize I even *had* a framework for what I do until I needed to organize the chapters for this Donkey Principle book.

What stopped me in my tracks was discovering that *it's been there all along*, guiding my work over the past ten years like a compass. It wasn't until I had a name (or acronym) for this "philosophy of transformation" that I could see the contours that had been shaping my work for years.

It was like tapping into a vein of gold. Oh, I'd been collecting nuggets along the way—hints that there was a source nearby—but suddenly I hit the mother lode that will continue to transform my life and work in a greater way. For this, I have you—my readers—to thank. In preparing a work for you, it turns out that *I've* been the recipient of an unexpected grace.

As you begin your own journey to embrace your inner donkey—that part of you that is willing to do the work of transformation so that you can create the kind of life and work you love—I pray that you will find *your* GOLD, that vein of wisdom that's been within you all along. There is a hidden trove of riches that runs through your life story, just like gold lying hidden in a mountain just waiting to be mined. It's been forged through your experiences, your difficulties, and your challenges. It's been refined in your tragedies and triumphs.

No one can take it from you, but you must stake a claim for yourself.

I believe that you have been given your own mine filled with wisdom, a knack for making your way, and resilience that will carry you through the arduous task of bringing your gold to the light of day in order to bless the world. This is your Imago Dei, the divine spark that graces your life as a human being made in the image of God.

So go ahead:

Give yourself permission: Ask questions and aspire to be your truest, bravest, and goodest self.

Own your story: Your past, your present, and your people. Be honest about your assumptions and how they shape your actions in unintended ways. Take responsibility for your vision, voice, and values.

Lean in to your unique strengths: Assemble your team, remember your assets, and astound the world.

Deliver your work: Serve others in the special way that only you can. Choose a pace that works for you and set up systems that make serving meaningful and sustainable. Leave room for rest, play, and above all, joy.

What this world needs are fewer racehorses and more donkeys. Less spectacle and more substance. Service over show. Impact, not just entertainment.

This world needs *you*.

It needs what *you* bring to it.

You are made to live well for the long haul.

DISCUSSION QUESTIONS

INTRODUCTION

1. Have you ever been in a situation with a group of people where there were distinct social differences that made you uncomfortably vulnerable? Do you consider yourself a "misfit in limbo"?

CHAPTER 1: ASK

1. Were you curious as a child? Did someone encourage you to be curious? A parent? A teacher? Why do you think many people lose their curiosity as adults?

2. Does the question "Why not?" frighten you or stir up an adventurous spirit in you?

3. Did Margaret Knight's story get you thinking about possibilities in your life that you've shelved?

4. "What would" fantastical dreams don't have to be big and world changing. What small, personal fantastical dream tops your list? Why is it important to you?

5. Are you a schedule maker or a schedule breaker? Do you feel restricted by a schedule or liberated by one? Can a person have too much flexibility?

CHAPTER 2: ASPIRE

1. Had you ever heard this story about George Washington and King Charles III of Spain? Were you surprised by Washington's request?

2. Do you struggle with your own worthiness? How does your "outside you" differ from your "inside you"? Which one tends to overshadow the other?

3. Rachel suggested a list of roles a person could be good at, beginning with the phrase "Be a good _____." How would you fill in the blank? Have you ever surprised yourself or others with how good you are at something?

4. "Bravery asks us to trust." Is that difficult for you? What would help you overcome that struggle?

CHAPTER 3: ASCRIBE HONOR

1. Do you believe you have a divine story to tell? Who would you like to share it with?

2. Rachel encourages each reader to "honor your past" with a personalized ceremony. What would be an important detail you want to include?

3. "Be present to your present." What does that mean to you?

4. Whom do you consider "your people"? Why do you give them that designation? Have you experienced "one of your own" being honored in a special way?

CHAPTER 4: ASSUME

1. Did you have assumptions about donkeys before you began reading this book?

2. Have you ever been caught in an embarrassing situation like Rachel where, thankfully, you realized how wrong you were about someone before you actually said anything out loud?

3. Have you or anyone you know discovered untapped abilities during a time of desperation?

4. Do you consider yourself an empathetic and compassionate person? How have you been able to demonstrate that?

1. Were you familiar with the story of Baalam and his talking donkey? In it, a humble animal brought unexpected insight into the situation. Have your eyes ever been "opened" by an animal or something else in the natural world?

2. Have you ever thought of yourself as a visionary? Do you know anyone whom you would consider a visionary worth emulating?

3. Were you taught certain values as a child? If so, what were they? Why are values so important?

4. Who in the world represents an authentic voice for you today? What can you learn from them?

CHAPTER 6: ASSEMBLE

1. In the opening story, are you more like Siba or Zuni?

2. A person's heroes change over a lifetime. Can you think of people you looked up to at different times in your life?

3. How do you feel about networking? Have you had a good or bad experience with it?

4. Think about the people who make up your herd, those who really "get" you or your work. How would you describe your herd? What makes them special?

CHAPTER 7: ASSETS

1. Has someone in your life been a model of resilience? In what ways?

2. What makes "bouncing back" such a challenge?

3. Looking back, have there been opportunities you missed because you were afraid that they were too risky?

4. What is the longest you have stuck with something to reach a goal? How did you feel when you finally accomplished what you set out to do?

1. Did you ever read *Brighty of the Grand Canyon* when you were young? What do you remember most about the story? If you've never read it, are you inspired to find a copy?

2. Who would you love to prove wrong about who you are and what you are capable of achieving?

3. Who is the most remarkable person you know? What have you gleaned from that person's approach to life?

4. What do you think of Fred Rogers's concept of "sacred space" and how he was able to use it so effectively with children? Do you think it's easy to create a sacred space with adults? Why or why not?

CHAPTER 9: ASCEND

1. How would you describe your normal pace in life when it comes to getting things done? Rushing? Leisurely? Plodding?

2. Rachel introduces the idea of "pacing" and "packing." What are the benefits of each? What is the benefit of pairing them together?

3. Does listening to and following your instincts sound terrifying or empowering to you? What kind of presence do you want to be in the world?

4. When was the last time you paused to really ponder a decision? Do you think it made a difference to the outcome?

CHAPTER 10: ASSIST

1. What impressed you the most about Luis Soriano's story?

2. What qualities have you admired in a servant-like person? If you've participated in any service projects, what have you learned that could help you benefit others?

3. Have you ever been burned out by doing too much to help others? What lesson did you take from that experience?

4. When it comes to "doing it alone" or sharing the load with a team, which sounds more appealing to you?

CHAPTER 11: ASLEEP & ASWIRL

1. Did Rachel choose the best pièce de résistance donkey illustration to wrap up the book? If so, why do you think so?

2. Are you guilty of thinking of rest as a commodity that can be traded? Be honest. What got you into that mindset?

3. "Play deepens your sense of identity, gives you a community of like-minded people, and fuels your capacity—when it *is* time to work—to work harder and smarter." Do you agree with Rachel's statement? Have you ever considered how rewarding play can be? Will you ever look at play the same way again?

4. Have you experienced a joyful life? Are you ready to now?

CONCLUSION: ASTERISK

1. Rachel realizes that writing this book opened her eyes to truths that she didn't even know had been directing her for years. Can you attest to something similar in your life? Does Rachel's GOLD framework resonate with you?

ACKNOWLEDGMENTS

This is the part where I get to ascribe honor to the people who have made this book possible!

Thanks always to my husband, Tom, for his unending encouragement to write what's in my heart; and to our kids and their spouses (Lauren and Robert Penn, Meghan and Nathan Miller, and Grayson and Emily Ridge), who continually cheer me on from the sidelines. My heart is overjoyed just thinking about you and the ways you love me, even when my head is in the clouds.

My magnificent team at Tyndale has outdone themselves with this book. My publisher, Sarah Atkinson, who never wavers in her enthusiasm for my donkey stories; and Christina Garrison, my acquisitions editor, both "got" my vision from the beginning. I am deeply grateful for Bonne Steffen, who polishes my words and finds the heart of what I'm trying to say. I love working with her. Annette Hayward, my copy editor, is great at seeing what I've missed, and her suggestions make it that much better. The art direction provided by Dean Renninger and the *incredible* cover and interior design by Libby Dykstra truly bring *The Donkey Principle* to life. I absolutely fell over when I first saw this cover, and I still can't get over it, Libby! Typesetter Laura Cruise took on the challenge of this book with style. Thanks also to the production team, Megan Alexander and Raquel Corbin, along with Kristi Gravemann and Kristen Magnesen in Marketing and Katie Dodillet, my publicist. Every step along the way matters. Thank you all for your hard work—your resourcefulness, resilience, and resolve—to make this book shine like gold. I am grateful.

With love,

RACHEL

NOTES

page 16   ***"The important thing is not to stop questioning":*** William Miller,
           "Death of a Genius: His Fourth Dimension, Time, Overtakes
           Einstein," *Life* 38, no. 18, 64.

page 19   ***One of the first women to ever receive a patent:*** David Lindsay, *House
           of Invention: The Secret Life of Everyday Products* (Lanham MD, Lyons
           Press, 2002), 125–29.

page 33   ***"Requesting a personal favor for General George Washington":*** Find
           more about this story at José Emilio Yanes, "Royal Gift (Donkey),"
           George Washington's Mount Vernon (website), accessed April 27,
           2022, https://www.mountvernon.org/library/digitalhistory/digital
           -encyclopedia/article/royal-gift-donkey/; and Alexis Coe, "George
           Washington Saw a Future for America: Mules," *Smithsonian
           Magazine*, February 12, 2020, https://www.smithsonianmag.com
           /history/george-washington-saw-future-america-mules-180974182/.

page 38   ***"True belonging is the spiritual practice":*** Brené Brown, *Braving the
           Wilderness: The Quest for True Belonging and Courage to Stand Alone*
           (New York: Random House, 2019), 40, italics in the original.

page 42   ***Tom Shadyac, who was living "his best life":*** James Altuchner, "Tom
           Shadyac Had It All, and Gave It Away," *Observer*, April 15, 2014,
           https://observer.com/2014/04/tom-shadyac-had-it-all-and-gave-it-away/.

page 47   *"one of the best jazz interpreters":* "Changing Channels," *Washington Post*, June 9, 2019, https://www.washingtonpost.com/graphics/2019 /lifestyle/women-over-50/. See also http://www.bettyelavette.com /content/about.

page 53   *Feast of the Asses:* Patricia Kasten, "A Feast Day for the Humble Donkey," Compass, January 12, 2013, https://www.thecompassnews .org/2013/01/a-feast-day-for-the-humble-donkey/.

page 61   *"The meeting of two eternities":* Henry David Thoreau, *Walden* (Oxford: Oxford University Press, 1997), 17.

page 63   *It relieves stress and cultivates peace:* Robert Emmons, "Why Gratitude Is Good," *Greater Good Magazine*, November 16, 2010, https://greatergood.berkeley.edu/article/item/why_gratitude_is_good.

page 66   *most impactful act leaders and managers can do:* Magdalena Nowicka Mook, "Good Leaders Acknowledge Their Employees Often," *Harvard Business Review*, March 30, 2021, https://hbr.org/sponsored /2021/03/good-leaders-acknowledge-their-employees-often.

page 73   *Walt Disney is following the storyline:* Wikipedia, s.v. "Land of Toys," last modified October 7, 2021, 23:52, https://en.wikipedia.org/wiki /Land_of_Toys.

page 73   *"attitudes or stereotypes that affect our understanding":* Charlotte Ruhl, "Implicit or Unconscious Bias," Simply Psychology, July 1, 2020, https://www.simplypsychology.org/implicit-bias.html.

page 82   *Michelangelo was asked by Pope Julius II to paint:* Jennie Cohen, "7 Things You May Not Know about the Sistine Chapel," History, October 26, 2021, https://www.history.com/news/7-things-you-may -not-know-about-the-sistine-chapel.

page 85   *create freeways for positive thought patterns:* Courtney Ackerman, "What Is Neuroplasticity? A Psychologist Explains," Positive

Psychology, last updated March 28, 2022, https://positivepsychology
.com/neuroplasticity/.

page 89   *a celebrity magician named Balaam is in a rage:* The story of Balaam
           and his donkey (called Tahira here) is based on the biblical account of
           Balaam and his donkey found in Numbers 22.

page 93   *"Envisioning the future is not about gazing":* James M. Kouzes and
           Barry Z. Posner, *The Leadership Challenge* (Hoboken, NJ: Wiley &
           Sons, 2017), 103.

page 97   *"Leaders must openly and directly talk about integrity":* Robert
           Chesnut, "How to Build a Company That (Actually) Values Integrity,"
           Harvard Business Review, July 30, 2020, https://hbr.org/2020/07/how
           -to-build-a-company-that-actually-values-integrity.

page 112   *George Washington invested in Alexander Hamilton:* "Alexander
           Hamilton and His Patron, George Washington," PBS American
           Experience, accessed May 2, 2022, https://www.pbs.org/wgbh
           /americanexperience/features/hamilton-and-his-patron-george
           -washington/.

page 119   *Kristin Schell was a busy mom of four:* Kristin Schell, *The Turquoise
           Table: Finding Community and Connection in Your Own Front Yard*
           (Nashville, TN: Thomas Nelson, 2017). See also The Turquoise Table
           website at https://theturquoisetable.com/.

page 124   *"It is resilient, reliable and obstinate":* Mark Shannon, quoted in
           Rose Murray Brown, "The Donkey Grape," Rose Murray Brown
           Masterclass, March 11, 2016, https://www.rosemurraybrown.com
           /rose-uncut/articles/the-donkey-grape.

page 126   *Once upon a time, a young donkey asked his grandpa:* Harvey Mackay,
           "Be Resourceful to Be Successful," Des Moines Register, February 1,
           2015, https://www.desmoinesregister.com/story/money/business
           /columnists/2015/02/02/harvey-mackay-resourceful/22592569/.

page 128   *"It's not what happens to you, but how you handle":* Zig Ziglar, *Something to Smile About: Encouragement and Inspiration for Life's Ups and Downs* (Nashville, TN: Nelson, 1997), 33.

page 128   ***Mallory Weggemann, a young woman who became paralyzed:*** See Mallory Weggemann, *Limitless: The Power of Hope and Resilience to Overcome Circumstance* (Nashville, TN: Thomas Nelson, 2021).

page 132   ***let go from his job as an architect:*** Pat Flynn, *Let Go: How to Transform Moments of Panic into a Life of Profits and Purpose* (Flynnspired Productions, Audiobook version, 2016).

page 135   *"fixed or set in purpose or opinion;* **resolute**": *Random House Kernerman Webster's College Dictionary* (2010), s.v. "stubborn," accessed May 3, 2022, https://www.thefreedictionary.com/stubborn.

page 136   ***"perseverance and passion for long-term goals":*** Angela Duckworth website, FAQ: "What Is Grit?," accessed May 3, 2022, https://angeladuckworth.com/qa/.

page 136   *"Grit isn't about getting an incredible dose of inspiration":* James Clear, "Grit: A Complete Guide on Being Mentally Tough," accessed May 3, 2022, https://jamesclear.com/grit.

page 141   *a pig was getting syrup-drenched pancakes:* Laura Numeroff, *If You Give a Pig a Pancake*, illus. Felicia Bond (New York: HarperCollins, 1998).

page 146   ***Alison's improbable path allowed her to build a successful company:*** For more information, visit alisonlumbatis.com.

page 151   ***Bush was well known for his personal, handwritten letters:*** Nancy Olson, "George H. W. Bush's Life in Letters," *Forbes*, December 3, 2018, https://www.forbes.com/sites/nancyolson/2018/12/03/george-h-w-bushs-life-in-letters/?sh=56c47ac37fa5; see also George H. W. Bush, *All the Best, George Bush: My Life in Letters and Other Writings* (New York: Scribner, 2013).

page 162   *a founding member of the New Mexico Pack Burro team and a board member of the Western Pack Burro Ass-ociation:* See NM Pack Burros, nmpackburros.com, and the Western Pack Burro Ass-ociation website, https://www.packburroracing.org/board-members.

page 167   *"Understand what it really takes":* Dorie Clark, *The Long Game: How to Be a Long-Term Thinker in a Short-Term World* (Boston, MA: Harvard Business Review Press, 2021), 206.

page 170   *he became world-renowned for his photography:* Chase Jarvis, *Creative Calling: Establish a Daily Practice, Infuse Your World with Meaning, and Succeed in Work + Life* (New York: Harper Collins, 2019), 614.

page 170   *"The whisper of intuition telling us":* Jarvis, *Creative Calling,* 11.

page 171   *"Presence is the state of being attuned":* Amy Cuddy, *Presence: Bringing Your Boldest Self to Your Biggest Challenges* (New York: Little, Brown Spark, 2015); Audiobook version narrated by Amy Cuddy (Audible, 2021), 00:46:21-55.

page 179   *Alfa and Beto are the transporters for the "biblioburro":* Graham Keeley, "Meet Luis Soriano, the Spanish Teacher Bringing Books to Children in Rural Colombia by Donkey," iNews, September 24, 2021, https://inews.co.uk/news/world/meet-luis-soriano-spanish-teacher-colombia-bringing-books-children-donkey-library-1214835.

page 180   *the area's first-ever library in La Gloria:* Jordan Salama, "Luis Soriano Had a Dream, Two Donkeys, and a Lot of Books," Atlas Obscura, November 17, 2021, https://www.atlasobscura.com/articles/biblioburro-colombia.

page 182   *42 million working donkeys worldwide supporting . . . over 250 million people:* Stephanie L. Church, "Beasts of Burden," *The Horse,* accessed May 4, 2022, https://thehorse.com/features/beasts-of-burden-africas-working-horses-and-donkeys/; Freya Dowson, "Working Donkeys and Horses from around the World in Pictures,"

Guardian, December 22, 2015, https://www.theguardian.com/global
-development-professionals-network/gallery/2015/dec/22/working
-donkeys-and-horses-from-around-the-world-in-pictures.

page 183   ***born into a poor family in a remote village in Nepal:*** Ali Gripper, *The Barefoot Surgeon. The Inspirational Story of Dr Sanduk Ruit, the Eye Surgeon Giving Sight and Hope to the World's Poor* (Crows Nest, NSW, Australia: Allen & Unwin, 2018).

page 184   ***Meghan, an early childhood music specialist:*** See the Flourish Music Facebook page at https://www.facebook.com/flourishmusicclass/.

page 184   ***Kwesia, also known as @citygirlinnature:*** "A Case for the Transformational Power of Nature and Adventure," Now on Earth website, accessed May 4, 2020, https://www.nowonearth.com/story-city-girl -in-nature/. Learn more about Kwesia at citygirlinnature.com.

page 188   ***Brooke is a nonprofit organization that assists donkeys:*** Learn more about this worthy international nonprofit at https://www.thebrooke .org/.

page 201   ***"The best bridge between despair and hope":*** Matthew Walker, *Why We Sleep: Unlocking the Power of Sleep and Dreams* (New York: Scribner, Kindle version, 2017), 152.

page 201   ***Sleep deprivation is linked to issues like cardiovascular disease:*** Walker, *Why We Sleep*, 49.

page 202   ***Some famous nappers include Aristotle, Leonardo da Vinci:*** Elizabeth Scott, "The Overwhelming Benefits of Power Napping," Verywell Mind, January 2, 2020, https://www.verywellmind.com/power -napping-health-benefits-and-tips-stress-3144702; Victoria Webster, "11 Most Surprising Famous People Who Loved to Nap," Carousel,

February 5, 2022, https://thecarousel.com/health/11-most
-surprising-famous-people-who-loved-to-nap/.

page 204   *"play is so important":* Meredith Hodges, *Training Mules and Donkeys: A Logical Approach to Longears* (Las Vegas: Alpine Publishing, 1993), 16.

page 205   *opportunities for play create an atmosphere:* Jennifer Wallace, "Why It's Good for Grownups to Go Play," May 19, 2017, https://www .washingtonpost.com/national/health-science/why-its-good-for-grown -ups-to-go-play/2017/05/19/99810292-fd1f-11e6-8ebe-6e0dbe4f2bca _story.html.

page 205   *"We are built to play and built through play":* Stuart Brown, *Play: How It Shapes the Brain, Opens the Imagination, and Invigorates the Soul* (New York: Penguin, 2009), 5–6.

page 206   *play* at work *is linked with less fatigue:* "Playing Up the Benefits of Play at Work," Association for Psychological Science, October 13, 2017, https://www.psychologicalscience.org/news/minds-business /playing-up-the-benefits-of-play-at-work.html, emphasis added.

page 208   *"Find your purpose, and you will experience more joy":* Bob Goff, *Undistracted: Capture Your Purpose, Rediscover Your Joy* (Nashville: Thomas Nelson, 2022), 9.

page 209   *"Look!" said Jill suddenly:* C. S. Lewis, *The Last Battle* (New York: Harper Trophy, 1994), 190–91.

Rachel with her donkeys Flash and Henry

ABOUT THE AUTHOR

RACHEL ANNE RIDGE is an author, artist, and speaker who delights audiences with her books and motivational presentations. In the midst of the Great Recession she adopted a stray donkey, who became the inspiration to create lasting change that would propel her toward success "for the long haul." Rachel's bestselling book, *Flash: The Homeless Donkey Who Taught Me about Life, Faith, and Second Chances*, has been optioned as a movie. Her subsequent books, including *Walking with Henry: Big Lessons from a Little Donkey on Faith, Friendship, and Finding Your Path*, expand on her reputation as an engaging writer. A certified life coach, Rachel helps people and organizations to get unstuck by harnessing the power of their own possibilities. Learn more at rachelanneridge.com.

Trail Notes

_____

_____

_____

_____

_____

_____

_____

_____

_____

_____

_____

_____

_____

_____

_____

_____

_____

_____

_____

Also by Rachel Anne Ridge

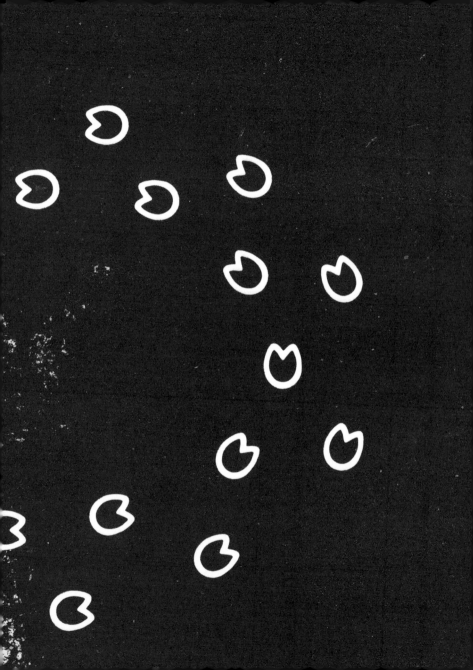